A garden
in a small
container

A forest
on a hill
of moss

KESHIKI BONSAI

A murmuring stream in a dish

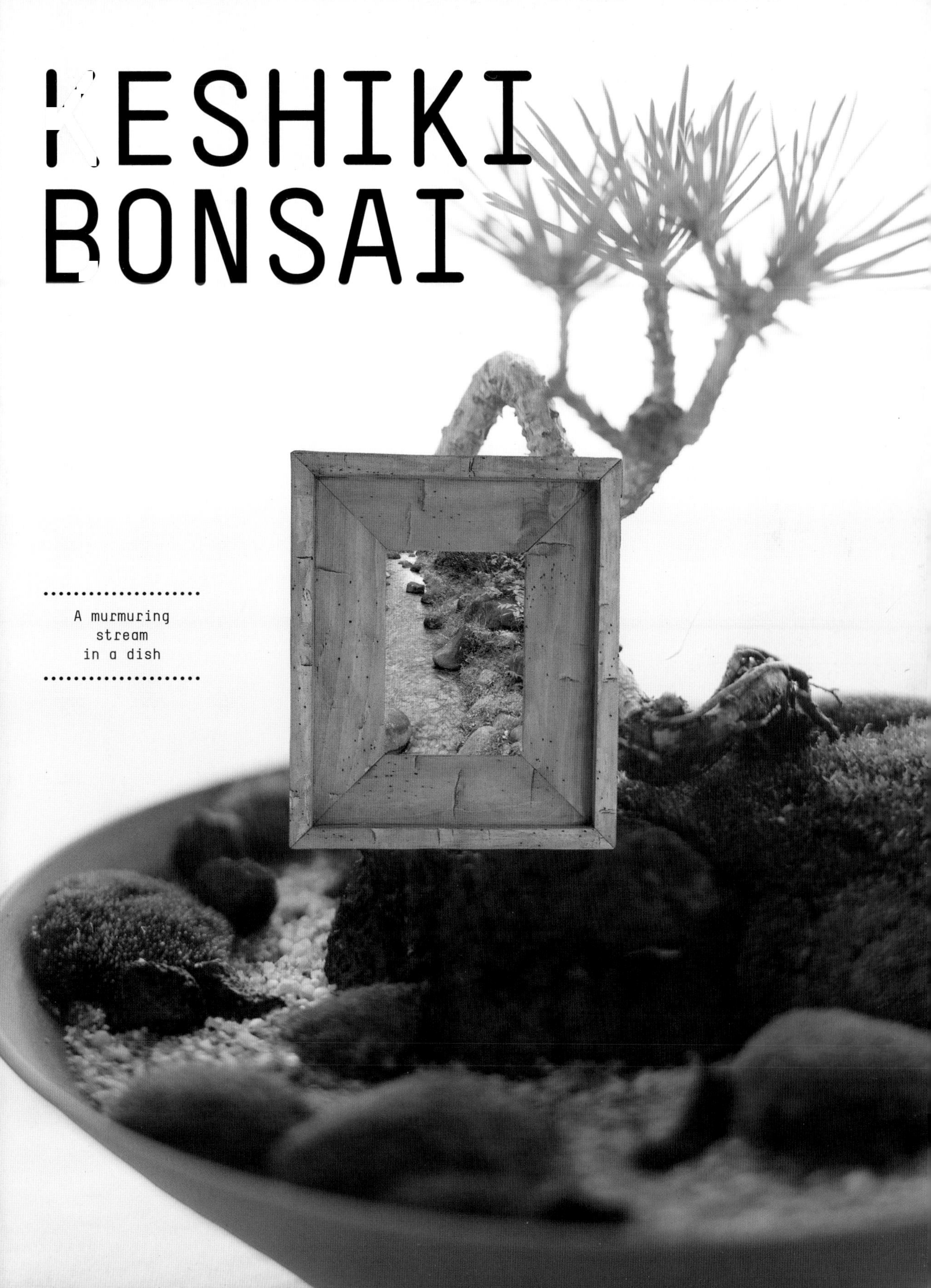

Original Japanese edition published
by Nitto Shoin Honsha Co., Ltd.

 This English
edition is published by arrangement
with Nitto Shoin Honsha Co., Ltd.,
Tokyo in care of Tuttle-Mori
Agency, Inc., Tokyo

Translation by Lynn Katsumoto

Design by Breanna Goodrow

Published in 2012
by Timber Press, Inc.

The Haseltine Building
133 S.W. Second Avenue, Suite 450
Portland, Oregon 97204-3527
timberpress.com

2 The Quadrant
135 Salusbury Road
London NW6 6RJ
timberpress.co.uk

Printed in China

Library of Congress Cataloging-in-Publication Data
Kobayashi, Kenji, 1970-
Keshiki bonsai : the easy, modern way to create miniature landscapes / Kenji Kobayashi. -- English language ed.
p. cm.
Original Japanese edition published by Nitto Shoin Honsha Co., Ltd. in 2007.
"Translation by Lynn Katsumoto."
Includes bibliographical references and index.
ISBN 978-1-60469-359-1
1. Bonsai. I. Title.
SB433.5.K59 2012
635.9'772--dc23

2012003234

A catalog record for this book is also available from the British Library.

Pages 1–3: Keshiki bonsai brings the four seasons inside your four walls.

KESHIKI BONSAI

The Easy, Modern Way to Create Miniature Landscapes

Kenji Kobayashi

Timber Press
PORTLAND / LONDON

CONTENTS

MOSS, TREES, PERENNIALS, AND STONES

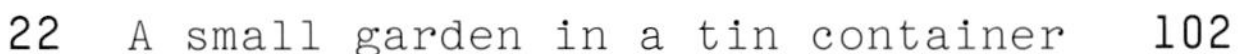

BONSAI IN NOVEL CONTAINERS

FOREWORD

Down a quiet backstreet in the tranquil Jiyugaoka neighborhood on the outskirts of Tokyo sits a tiny little plant shop with corrugated walls and shelves of potted plants. With no space for a formal garden, most people in urban Japan have cultivated every available centimeter of space in front of their homes and businesses for generations, attempting to keep the most modest suggestion of natural beauty in their daily lives. The sight of old folks pottering about with their plants endlessly at the side of the lane is an endearing memory of days gone by—a memory that young Kenji Kobayashi refused to let die.

My first visit to Kobayashi-san's contemporary bonsai shop, Sinajina (pronounced sheena-jeena), was in 2009, when I went in search of an artist whose reputation as one of Japan's top "green designers" had reverberated all the way across The Pond to Portland, Oregon, where I am curator of the Pavilion Gallery of the Portland Japanese Garden.

Winding my way down the narrow passageway beside the shop, past the rows of tiny plants and trays of thick green moss that comprise Sinajina nursery, I entered an elegantly simple space that served as Kobayashi-san's office, showroom, and classroom all in one. I recognized a certain air of Tokyo urban chic—bare tables of natural unfinished wood contrasting with metal and concrete as a foil for the fresh green of Kobayashi's remarkable miniature creations. Without the snobbery that sometimes accompanies purveyors of all that is fashionable, Kobayashi-san and his small staff greet their guests with a warm welcome and a cup of hot tea. Just like his lovable potted plants, Kobayashi-san himself somehow retains the spirit of the old world Japanese merchant, living and working on a quiet backstreet, focused on the quality and aesthetics of his products and on making "doing business" a warm personal experience.

Kobayashi invented the art of "keshiki bonsai," a new style of bonsai he developed himself—a style he believes fits the lifestyle of young city dwellers in Tokyo who have no space or time to devote to traditional bonsai, a practice that had come to be perceived as the elegant pursuit of retired gentlemen. Kobayashi understood the universal love of nature and saw the potential for new directions.

One would expect that Kobayashi first learned the art of bonsai in Japan, but the wonder of it all is that he traveled all the way to Portland, Oregon, in the 1980s to find Masa Furukawa, the bonsai teacher who was to open his eyes to new possibilities for bringing nature into people's lives in the twenty-first century. Furukawa sensei introduced Kobayashi to a little-known branch of bonsai called saikei, a simpler style of bonsai developed after World War II by bonsai master Toshio Kawamoto as a way to create miniature potted landscapes using young seedlings rather than the more elaborately cultivated single specimen trees used in traditional bonsai that require generations of time to bring to maturity. By studying outside of Japan with Mr. Furukawa, Kobayashi says he learned traditional techniques but with greater freedom to imagine his own style.

In 1998, he opened Sinajina and began to reinvent and simplify traditional saikei landscapes even further, developing a method of teaching Tokyo city dwellers how to create and maintain them. With a designer's eye, Kobayashi worked with ceramists and metal craftsmen as well as local nurserymen to create a modern imaginary world in plants.

His keshiki bonsai capture a tiny glimpse of nature using young seedlings, grasses, and moss in a container often barely larger than a teacup. His diminutive creations are perfect for the modern city dweller—they take very little time to make, they fit on the tiniest window ledge, and they require just a moment or two of attention to care for each day. Filled to the brim with a thick carpet of moss, these pots might contain a single Japanese beech seedling with a gently off-center curve to its still burgeoning branches, or a tiny clump of mondo grass. Sometimes the featured greenery is the lush moss itself surrounded only by a curving "stream" of sand to suggest the flow of water around a mossy riverbank.

In 2010, the international appeal of Kobayashi-san's approach was demonstrated by a special exhibition of more than thirty-five keshiki bonsai created on-site at the Portland Japanese Garden as part of the Art in the Garden series of annual exhibitions. For his materials, he foraged locally for small plants, grasses, and moss. The containers included a selection of his own signature round bonsai pots, as well as a number that were handmade by twelve local potters of the Oregon Potters Association for this exhibition, bringing both cultures together in this project.

Today, Kobayashi enjoys tremendous success in Tokyo with his new style of urban green. His work now graces the walls, indoor gardens, and countertops of fashionable restaurants and chic boutiques throughout Japan, bringing a bit of green back into the lives of his twenty-first-century audience.

There is much discussion of the great traditions of Japan disappearing one by one in the face of the modernization (read: Westernization) that has unquestionably changed forever the complexion of urban Japan. But the good news is that a few young artists like Kenji Kobayashi understand that tradition is about picking up the thread of continuity with the past—not about staying the same. They are carrying on the spirit of the old ways, creating a new tradition of their own that continues to treasure the beauty of nature and understands the way it enriches the lives of people today, no matter where they find themselves.

In the pages that follow, Kobayashi-san shows thirty-seven finished bonsai and gives careful step-by-step instructions on how to create them. Perhaps even more important, each project is inspired by Kobayashi-san's vision of nature and unique approach to his art. This spirit is bound to win him new admirers in the English-speaking world and enrich the lives of all who are touched by it.

Diane Durston
Curator of Culture, Art, and Education
Portland Japanese Garden

PREFACE

Bonsai literally means a planting (*sai*) that is nurtured in a tray or planter (*bon*). In Japan, bonsai has a long history going back as far as the Heian period (794 –1185) when envoys from China are said to have introduced the art. Today, people all over the world have become captive to its charms. In fact, I traveled to America to learn the art of bonsai. While there, I began to realize that bonsai has taken on a stylish new image that appeals to people interested in design and the arts.

In Japan, there is a preconceived notion that bonsai is an expensive pastime for the senior citizen. Bonsai suffers from being considered a complicated hobby, a high-maintenance sibling of elaborate gardening. Indeed, I was one of those people who thought of bonsai as a stale, excessively intricate diversion for those with too much time on their hands. What first got me interested in the world of bonsai was a photograph I saw in a book by Toshio Kawamoto called *Ki to ishi no dezain*

(Designing with Trees and Stones). It showed cedar trees planted in a flat container, but what was remarkable was that the scale tricked the eye into believing that the picture had been shot from nature. The illusion was so strong, I felt like I was about to walk into a real forest. I still cannot forget my amazement that trees, rocks, and moss could evoke such a vibrant world in a single container.

The pleasure of composing a form that conjures nature in all its grandeur and yet is contained in just a small vessel rests in recreating and building a remembered landscape—say, a mountain seen in one's youth or a scene glimpsed on a trip—with plants and stones. As the plants develop, the four seasons reveal themselves through changes in foliage, and you find yourself immersed in the unfolding of nature. That's why I call my bonsai *keshiki* (landscape) bonsai. Even one pine, placed on top of a little hill of moss, presents a year-round communion with the living essence of scenery.

A miniature bonsai can pack a dynamic punch far exceeding its tiny footprint when placed thoughtfully in an interior. Consider it like an evolving work of art and let it serve as an element of decor. Cultivating an appreciation of the natural landscape is an acquired skill, like choosing the right wine to go with hors d'oeuvres.

Bonsai need not be associated solely with Japanese style. Instead, I'd like to see bonsai incorporated into your home as part of your living environment. It is with that goal in mind that I offer this book to introduce you to all there is to know about making the miniature bonsai landscapes that I have come to love. I've included bonsai terminology throughout the book to help you understand some technical terms that you may encounter in the world of miniature plant cultivation. Look through the photographs and then start with a container that you particularly adore.

If this book serves to inspire just one more bonsai fan, whether old or young, male or female, I will have fulfilled my deepest wish.

Kenji Kobayashi

Keshiki bonsai adds a fresh touch to any style of interior decor.

MINIMALIST STYLE

EURO STYLE

RUSTIC STYLE

JAPANESE STYLE

BASICS OF KESHIKI BONSAI

SOILS

While it would be best to use the soil of the place where the plant came from as the soil for keshiki bonsai, this is generally not possible. Instead, we need to make a mixture of soil that is right for most plants and that can absorb water but also let it drain. For the beginner, the bonsai soils available at garden supply or bonsai specialty shops provide a useful, convenient option.

SMALL-GRAIN AKADAMA, a volcanic soil, forms the base for bonsai potting soils. Akadama is available in large, medium, and small grain; small is what we use for basic soil mixtures.

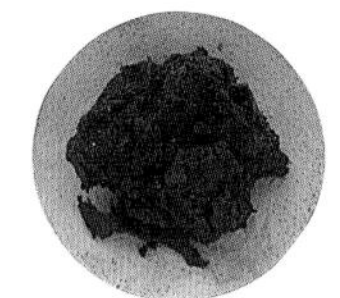

KETO (peat clay) is a soil derived from the deposits of decomposing plants that grow by the water. This soil is great for retaining water and fertilizer. Besides being beneficial in mixtures, keto is the ideal medium for a plant right after root washing.

FINE-GRAIN FUJI SAND has good water drainage and a nice black color. Besides being used in soil mixtures, Fuji sand is also good as a decorative topdressing.

COARSE-GRAIN FUJI SAND is useful as a subsoil and is in fact volcanic ash gathered from Mount Fuji. Air and water move through it well, making it good to use in the bottom of the container.

Before you undertake your first keshiki bonsai project, you need to know about soils and tools to have on hand. Many of the products mentioned here are available from suppliers of bonsai materials. This section also includes some tips on planting and care of your landscape bonsai.

MAKE A POTTING MIXTURE

It's a good idea to make a potting mixture beforehand. The benefit of mixing up a composite soil in advance is that it will be ready to use right when you need it. All of the soils used in this book are potting mixtures.

Combine three parts small-grain akadama, one part keto, and one part fine-grain Fuji sand and mix them together well. Then mix in a slow-release fertilizer such as MagAmp (magnesium ammonium phosphate), using the amount indicated on the package in proportion to the amount of soil.

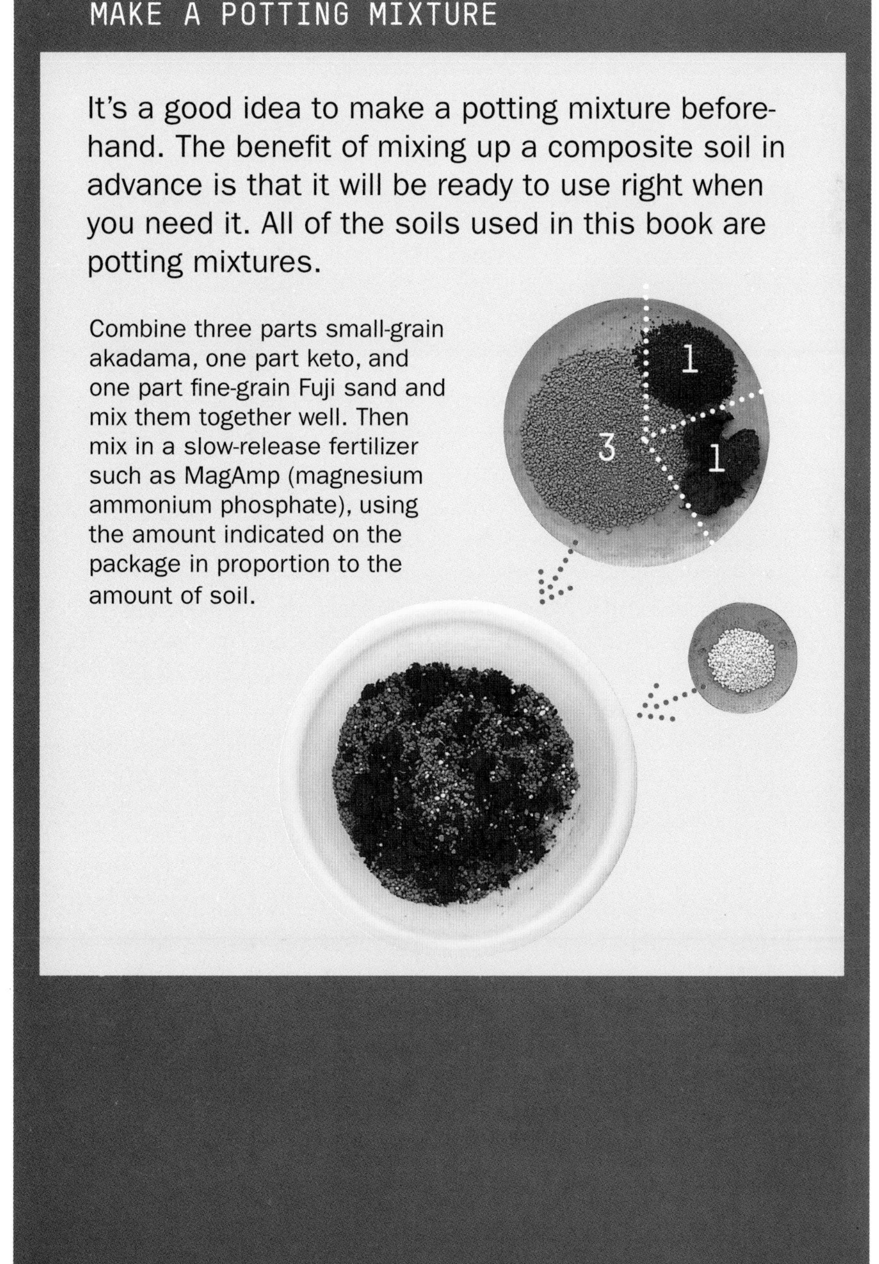

BASIC TOOLS

These are the essential tools for creating keshiki bonsai.

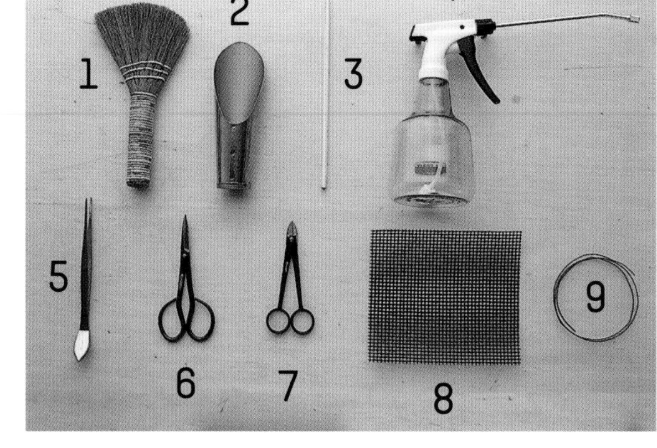

1. **HAND BROOM.** Handy for cleaning up soil and sand that falls onto the work area. Cleans without scratching the table. Use light, gentle strokes to brush dirt away.
2. **SCOOP.** Use for pouring soil into the container. Scoops come in many sizes, but use a small one for miniature bonsai. A narrow cylindrical shape is convenient for filling gaps in the soil.
3. **DISPOSABLE CHOPSTICKS.** Use for shaking off soil that is clinging to roots, and for filling gaps with soil after placing soil in the container.
4. **PLANT MISTER.** This type of sprayer works even when held at a slant. The nozzle is long so that the mist can reach to the back of the plant and spray evenly.
5. **TWEEZERS WITH SPATULA.** The spatula is for tamping the soil flat. The tweezers are good for untangling roots and removing small leaves. You can use a butter knife in place of a spatula.
6. **BONSAI SCISSORS.** Useful for cutting wood and old moss. These special scissors make delicate snips much easier because they are designed to grip well.
7. **WIRE CUTTERS.** In this book, the cutters are used to cut the aluminum wire holding the mesh on the bottom of the container. They are also useful when working with wire for shaping and styling trees.
8. **DRAINAGE MESH.** Covers the hole in the bottom of the container to keep soil from spilling out and insects from getting in. Cut the mesh with scissors to fit the size of the hole.
9. **ALUMINUM WIRE.** This is for securing the mesh in the bottom of the container. In this book, we will be using wire that is 1.5 mm in diameter. It is also used to wrap trees to style them into the right shape.

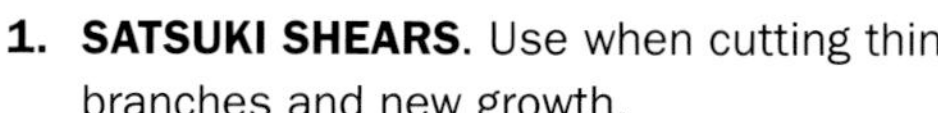

ADDITIONAL TOOLS

These additional tools are nice to have.

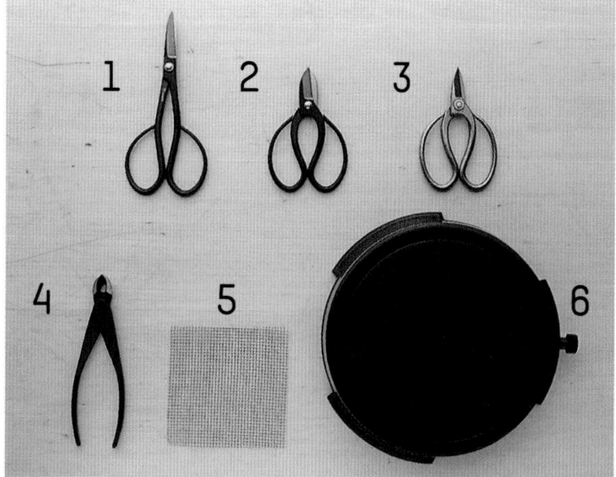

1. **SATSUKI SHEARS.** Use when cutting thin branches and new growth.
2. **MINI FLOWER SHEARS (copper).** The sturdy blades are good for cutting through thick pieces of wood. Some care needs to be taken since the blades are copper and will rust if not properly tended.
3. **MINI FLOWER SHEARS (stainless steel).** The thin blades are good for cutting small branches and flowers. The stainless steel blades are less prone to rusting, which is an advantage.
4. **BRANCH CUTTER.** The blades are short and very sharp, making it easier to cut branches in hard-to-reach places.
5. **COPPER NETTING (100 percent copper).** The metal ions in copper act as a repellent that keeps worms and slugs away from the container.
6. **TURNTABLE STAND (with stopper).** Lets you work by simply turning the table rather than needing to move the container. The stopper lets you stabilize the table at any position you want.

PLANTING TIPS

Here are some tips on how to proceed as you plant your own bonsai. I will point out things to watch for as we go along.

SECURE THE MESH IN THE BOTTOM OF THE PLANTER. The drainage hole in the bottom of the container provides a way for water to run off after you've watered the plants. If the opening is left the way it is, soil will spill out and pests can crawl in. You will secure mesh over the hole to prevent that.

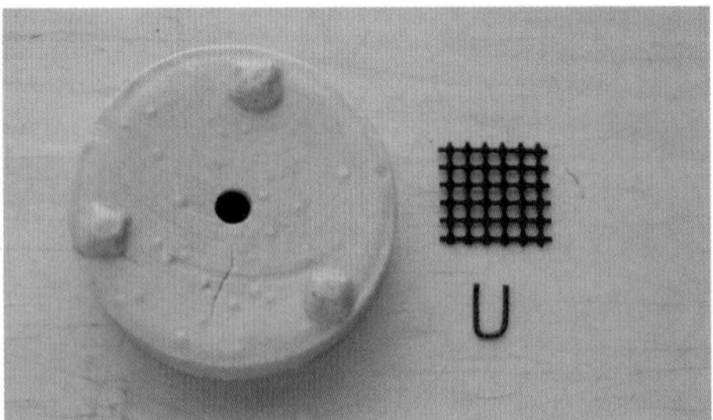

Cut the mesh to a size slightly larger than the drainage hole. Then cut a section of aluminum wire about 1¼ inches long and bend it into a U shape.

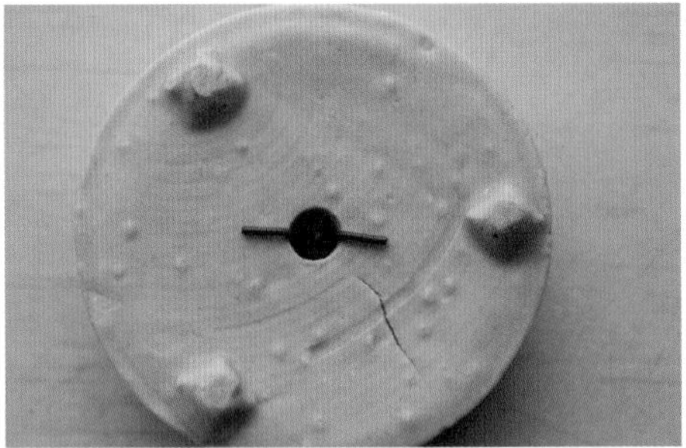

Push the U-shaped wire through the mesh and lay the mesh on top of the drainage hole so that it covers it. Next, pull the ends of the wire through the hole and bend them across the bottom of the container, as shown in the photograph.

REMOVE THE SOIL FROM POTTED SEEDLINGS. You will need to take the plant out of the container it came in and use tweezers to remove the soil from the surface and roots.

Often, the soil holding the seedlings you buy will have sprouts or weeds growing alongside. Use the tweezers to scrape the weeds away, since they will vie for nutrients if allowed to grow.

The soil clinging to the roots can be cleaned off using the tweezers to untangle the snarls. Excess roots can then be cut.

WASH THE ROOTS OF DELICATE PLANTS. Delicate plants with thin roots are best cleaned in water, not with tweezers, to remove soil. This is called ne arai, washing the roots. Take the seedling out of the pot and place it in a container of water. Carefully remove soil with the tips of your fingers, and then lay the plant on a cloth to remove the excess water. The seedling is then ready to be planted. If there are flowers blossoming or fruit on the branches, refrain from using this method since it will interrupt the flow of nutrients.

Place water in a bucket or bowl and put the roots in. Use your fingertip to coax the soil away from the roots.

When you have managed to clean the roots as shown here, you are finished.

Take the corner of an old towel that you have moistened and wrung excess water from, and fold it. Place the seedling on this. Then fold more of the towel on top to absorb the water.

DISCARD OLD MOSS. The black area on the back of a clump of moss, while it looks like soil, is actually old moss. Be sure to remove this by hand or with scissors before using the moss in bonsai.

Take the clump of moss that you want to use in your hand and turn it over. Pinch out about ¼ inch of old moss using your finger. For finely textured moss, such as velvet moss (birodogoke), use scissors to cut.

CARING FOR KESHIKI BONSAI

It is important to take care of keshiki bonsai every day—making sure, for instance, that it is in a good location, and giving it water and fertilizer—so that you can enjoy it for a long time. There are three basics for plant care: light, moisture, and nutrients. As you would take care of a child, be attentive to the appearance of your plants and take care of them to maintain their vibrant good health.

PLACEMENT. Some plants like light while others like shade. In general, let plants get two to three hours of sun per day, avoiding the strong sunlight of summer and western exposure. In the summer, protect the plants by lowering shades or blinds, or place them where there is a roof or awning to shade them. If you are keeping the bonsai indoors, place it near a window where it will get sunlight from morning until about 2:00 in the afternoon. Be sure to keep it in a room that is well used, since the simple presence of people brings moisture to the air. Outside on a veranda or patio, the heat from reflected light can easily dry the container out. Refrain from placing the container directly on concrete; let the container rest on bricks, a planter shelf, or a bench.

REPOTTING. Your plant will grow even in a small container. If you keep it there, the container will fill with roots and the trunk will weaken. Once you notice roots growing out of the bottom of the container and a decrease in how much water is absorbed, it is time for repotting. Generally, this needs to be done once every two or three years. Timing is critical to the success of repotting: avoid doing it in wintertime, when the roots are dormant. Early spring (February to March) is best since that is just before the roots begin to get active. Replace the soil, trim the overly long roots, and let new sprouts appear. For those plants with roots that can be separated, this is your chance to start a new container. Or you can repot in the same container if you trim long roots to half their length.

REMOVING AND PREVENTING PESTS. Over the course of the year, you will see the most marked increase in pests during the winter. Observe your plants carefully every day. If you see a bug, catch it by hand or with tweezers and remove it. If you still see insect damage, you may decide to use a pesticide. Whether you use an organic pesticide such as insecticidal soap or a synthetic pesticide, follow the instructions carefully. This is especially important in an indoor environment.

WATERING. Remember that the small container used for mini bonsai dries out quickly, so be conscientious about replenishing moisture. The general rule of thumb is to water well when the surface of the soil is dry, adding water until it flows out from the bottom. In the spring and fall, water once a day; in the summer, twice a day—morning and evening; and in the winter, water every other day in the morning and avoid watering at night, since it can freeze and damage the roots. Use a watering can with a rose (a cap with small holes) so that you can water the entire plant. A plant mister is also handy for keeping moss moist since moss absorbs water through its leaves.

FERTILIZER. The small size of the container for mini bonsai means that the plant will weaken if too much fertilizer is applied. If you use a slow-release type, you can dissolve it in water and apply in late winter to plants that flower in spring, and in late summer to plants that flower in autumn. Once the blossoms appear, switch to a liquid fertilizer and use once every two weeks. Follow the instructions on the label for the right proportions. There are also spray fertilizers that can be used on your plants every day without diluting. Some growers also like to use concentrated nonfertilizer stimulants to promote the plant's health and vigor. These must be diluted following the directions.

Keshiki bonsai in my own living space

I come from a family involved in the building business and grew up learning from my father that "to build a house is to make a home. You only have a home once you have both house and garden." With that in mind, my younger brother studied architecture and I went to school to learn landscape architecture, after which I worked in a garden design office. While drawing up plans I found myself wanting to work with actual plants in full scale, rather than just on flat pieces of paper.

It was around that time that I encountered the art of saike (planted scenery)—a landscape growing inside a shallow bowl. The work of recreating a beautiful landscape in a small container, surprisingly dynamic and at the same time delicate, spoke strongly to me. Many days passed while I was utterly absorbed in making bonsai, and at some point I became a captive of the art. I went all the way to the United States to study with a teacher living there, and my image of what bonsai is changed from what it had been in Japan. I realized that bonsai can be a stylish pursuit and that it can be enjoyed as an art form.

After returning to Japan, I searched for a personal style that would make use of the planted scenery that I'd learned, and some of the things that I made at the company where I was working drew people's attention. Then in 2002 I became the owner of a shop called Sinajina, specializing in modern crafts for the home, and I have been working for myself ever since. I established keshiki bonsai as a way to immerse oneself in the feeling of nature's flow while living a mostly indoor urban life, all of which has started me on an entirely new chapter of my life.

Both in my shop and in my private space, I have surrounded myself with keshiki bonsai. I am fond of well-worn northern European furniture and have discovered that keshiki bonsai looks great next to old, weathered wooden things. In fact, the little pots of styled foliage blend seamlessly with all styles of interior design. Just looking at a small potted landscape brings a measure of glorious calm. I can feel the stress melt away, and for a blissful moment it's possible to indulge in the full satisfaction of the finest tea or coffee. For me, an added pleasure is choosing the perfect cup for the beverage from my ceramics collection. Mind and body relax, while the senses delight in the pleasures of color, taste, and texture.

My collection of beverage containers includes sake cups and teacups by Omura Tsuyoshi, Ando Masanobu, Murakami Yaku, and Tanaka Nobuhiko that I particularly treasure. I've chosen them for their interesting shapes and their earthiness.

A keshiki bonsai of Japanese maple or momiji is placed on top of a northern European chest. A handsome textile beneath the container accents the scenic quality of the maple.

A simple hand towel printed with a traditional Japanese pattern sets off a moss bonsai on the dining table.

Simply a place to sleep, my house is decorated with a minimum amount of color, but I have placed items of furniture that I enjoy to create a tranquil space.

MOSS

There is nothing like moss for conveying the sense of undulating earth—its breadth, its depth, and the play of light and shade. Even a single clump of moss evokes the boundless pleasure of natural beauty, conjuring the feeling of mountain or forest scenery in a small container.

A play of
textures between
Japanese paper
and moss

KESHIKI 1

JAPANESE STYLE

 Japanese mountain moss (yamagoke)

2 inches in diameter by 1 inch tall

1 Thread aluminum wire through a piece of mesh placed in the bottom of the planter and pull the ends of the wire through the drainage hole, securing by bending the ends across the bottom.

2 Add enough coarse-grain Fuji sand to cover the mesh.

A tiny cup of moss, just big enough to fit in the palm of your hand, rests on a richly textured piece of Japanese paper (washi). The fibers you get when you tear the paper by hand enliven the composition.

3 Add enough potting mixture to nearly fill the planter, up to about 1/4 inch from the rim.

4 Use the plant mister to dampen the soil while tamping down and flattening it with the spatula. The soil will become slightly claylike, giving the moss a good base to stick to and helping it to establish quickly.

5 Use your fingers to pinch away old moss from the underside.

CHOKUKAN: A CONFIGURATION IN WHICH THE TRUNK RISES STRAIGHT UP FROM THE ROOT.

6 Separate the moss into many small pieces. Fit the pieces together like a puzzle and pat into place.

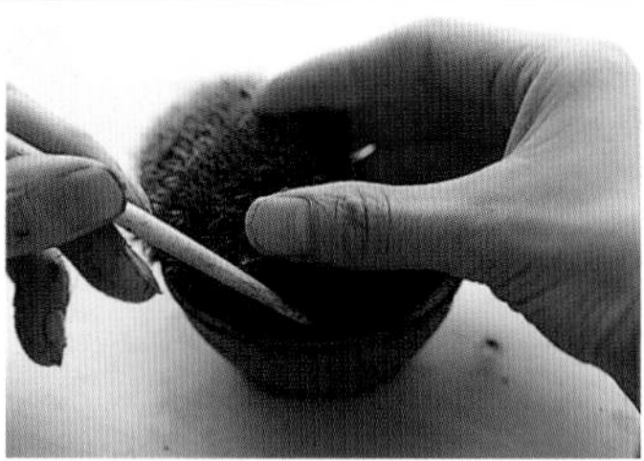

7 Use a chopstick to press back inside any moss hanging over the edge of the planter, keeping your fingers gently on the moss to hold it in place. Imagine that you are making a small hill. Finish by spraying with water.

DIFFERENT VARIETIES OF MOSS

Moss comes in many different textures, colors, and shapes. When making a landscape, select the type that presents the appearance you want in order to create a setting that is rich in natural beauty.

1. **VELVET MOSS (birodogoke).** Color is a deep, fresh green. Very fine texture, spreading luxuriantly like a plush carpet. Complements any type of landscape arrangement.

2. **CREEPING MOSS.** A hearty variety of moss that is often found growing on stone walls and other garden areas, forming matlike clusters. Prefers sunny locales. Leaves twist upward when the plant is dry.

3. **SAND MOSS (sunagoke).** A moss of delicate beauty that seems to be studded with stars. Best planted in a locale with good sunlight; quite resistant to both heat and dry conditions. Easy for beginners to work with.

4. **GRAY MOSS/MOUNTAIN LICHEN (araha okina goke).** Light greenish-yellow when the plant has dried out; dark green when excessively dampened. Leaves turn white when dry, so this moss is also known as white hair lichen. Highly valued and appreciated, this type of moss is prevalent at Saihoji, a temple in Kyoto, Japan, informally known as Kokedera or the moss temple.

5. **JAPANESE MOUNTAIN MOSS (yamagoke).** Intense green when it has absorbed a lot of moisture; gets lighter and lighter as it dries out. In nature, found most frequently on fallen and living trees; very resilient against drying out.

KESHIKI 2

A trio of tiny mosses all in a row

Small planters lined up in a row on a kitchen shelf bask in a sunny window. The warmth of the wood and the light shining through the window make the moss luminous.

MINIMALIST STYLE

velvet moss (birodogoke)

1¼ inches in diameter by ¾ inch tall

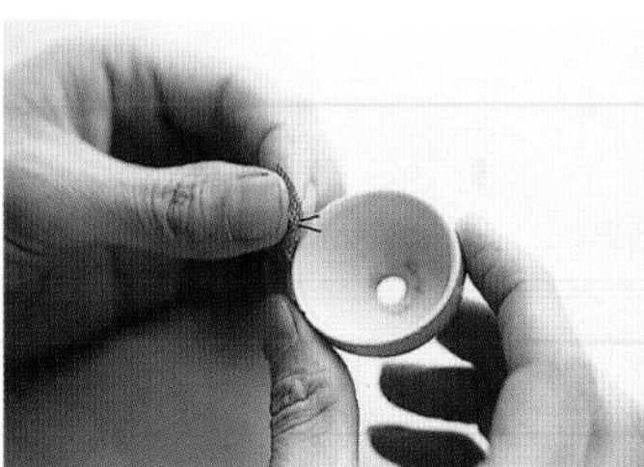

1 Thread aluminum wire through a piece of mesh placed in the bottom of the first planter and pull the ends of the wire through the drainage hole, securing by bending the ends across the bottom. Prepare the other two planters in the same way.

2 Add enough coarse-grain Fuji sand to cover the mesh in each planter.

3 Add enough potting mixture to nearly fill each planter, up to about 1/4 inch from the rim.

4 Use the plant mister to dampen the soil while tamping down and flattening it with the spatula. The soil will become slightly claylike, giving the moss a good base to stick to and helping it to establish quickly.

5 Use scissors to cut away old moss from the underside. This type of moss is so fine that it is hard to grab hold of by hand.

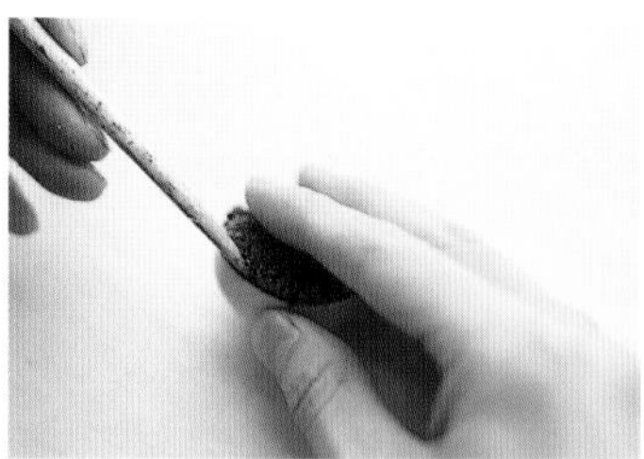

6 Pat the moss onto the soil and use a chopstick to press back inside any moss hanging over the edge of each planter, keeping your fingers gently on the moss to hold it in place. Imagine that you are making a small hill. Finish by spraying with water.

KESHIKI 3

Moss in
a contrasting
patterned
container

This bonsai may be small, but it has real presence. The contrast between the indigo in the container's pattern and the green of the moss pleases the eye. Even just one planter on a table brings a soothing calm to the atmosphere.

EURO STYLE

Japanese mountain moss (yamagoke)

2 inches by 2 inches by 2¼ inches tall

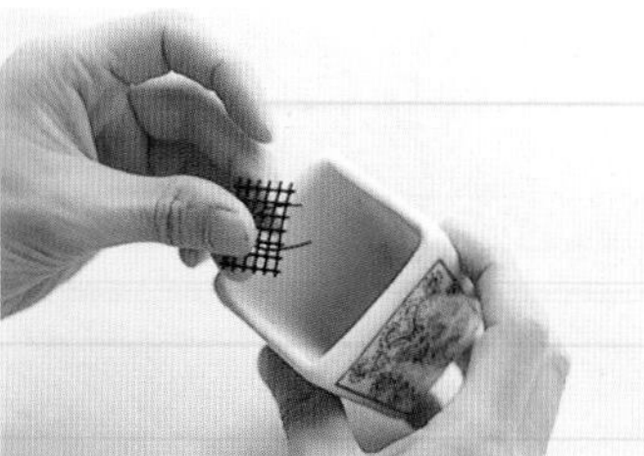

1 Thread aluminum wire through a piece of mesh placed in the bottom of the planter and pull the ends of the wire through the drainage hole, securing by bending the ends across the bottom.

2 Add enough coarse-grain Fuji sand to cover the mesh.

3 Add enough potting mixture to nearly fill the planter, up to about 1/4 inch from the rim.

4 Use the plant mister to dampen the soil while tamping down and flattening it with the spatula. The soil will become slightly claylike, giving the moss a good base to stick to and helping it to establish quickly.

5 Take a piece of moss that is slightly larger than the mouth of the container and use your fingers to pinch away old moss from the underside.

6 Put the moss on the soil and pat into place.

7 Use a chopstick to press back inside any moss hanging over the edge of the planter, keeping your fingers gently on the moss to hold it in place. Imagine that you are making a small hill. Finish by spraying with water.

KESHIKI 4

Red and green:
Christmas colors

Moss in bright red containers makes a fresh and clean accent against white tile on a countertop. The kitchen becomes a stress-free zone for making meals.

MINIMALIST STYLE

Japanese mountain moss (yamagoke)

1¼ inches by 1¼ inches by 2 inches tall

2 inches by 1¼ inches by 1 inch tall

1 Thread aluminum wire through a piece of mesh placed in the bottom of the first planter and pull the ends of the wire through the drainage hole, securing by bending the ends across the bottom. Prepare the other planter in the same way.

2 Add enough coarse-grain Fuji sand to cover the mesh in each planter.

3 Add enough potting mixture to nearly fill each planter, up to about 1/4 inch from the rim.

4 Use the plant mister to dampen the soil while tamping down and flattening it with the spatula. The soil will become slightly claylike, giving the moss a good base to stick to and helping it to establish quickly.

5 For each planter, take a piece of moss that is slightly larger than the mouth of the container and use your fingers to pinch away old moss from the underside.

6 Pat the moss onto the soil and use a chopstick to press back inside any moss hanging over the edge of each planter, keeping your fingers gently on the moss to hold it in place. Imagine that you are making a small hill. Finish by spraying with water.

SELECTING MOSS

While you might think that a fresh-looking, lustrous green moss is healthy and moss with bands of brown running through it is unhealthy, that is not always the case. Even moss that looks dried out can revive once it takes hold and grows in good soil.

Even moss that has turned brown is not necessarily unhealthy or dead. Both of these are acceptable.

CHOKUKON: A THICK ROOT THAT DESCENDS STRAIGHT DOWN FROM THE ROOT BASE.

KESHIKI 5

Moss in a square
container with
a layer-cake pattern

RUSTIC STYLE

 velvet moss (birodogoke)

1⅓ inches by 1⅓ inches by 1½ inches tall

1 Thread aluminum wire through a piece of mesh placed in the bottom of the planter and pull the ends of the wire through the drainage hole, securing by bending the ends across the bottom.

Moss in a square container with a pattern like Baumkuchen—a cake made in thin concentric layers that resemble tree rings, popular in Europe and Japan—is a perfect match for treasured objects that have been handed down through time. Amid an array of softly worn textures, the moss attracts the eye with its unexpected pop of soft color.

2 Add enough coarse-grain Fuji sand to cover the mesh.

3 Add enough potting mixture to nearly fill the planter, up to about 1/4 inch from the rim.

DAN-ISHI: A STONE WITH A SHAPE THAT SUGGESTS FLAT KNOLLS STACKED IN A STAIRCASE FORMATION.

4 Poke the soil with a chopstick to release air and remove any pockets. Jab many times to make a solid foundation of soil.

5 Use the plant mister to dampen the soil while tamping down and flattening it with the spatula. The soil will become slightly claylike, giving the moss a good base to stick to and helping it to establish quickly.

6 Take a piece of moss slightly larger than the mouth of the container and use your fingers to pinch away old moss from the underside.

7 Pat the moss onto the soil and use a chopstick to press back inside any moss hanging over the edge of the planter, keeping your fingers gently on the moss to hold it in place. Imagine that you are making a small hill. Finish by spraying with water.

TAKING CARE OF MOSS

Moss roots have no other role than to keep the plant secure in soil; moisture is absorbed not through the roots but through the surface of the leaves. If using moss soon, moisten it with water and let it sit on a sheet of newspaper. If you are not going to use it right away, form it into a ball, place it in a clear bag, and let it dry out. It can be left that way and still be fine after a year. Thirty minutes before using it, immerse it in water and then place it on the soil. Be sure to spray moss in keshiki bonsai frequently to replenish moisture.

Moisten moss with water and let it sit on a sheet of newspaper if you will be using it soon, or form it into a ball and store it in a clear bag for later use.

DOHA: WAVES OR SLOPES FORMED BY SOIL.

EDA UCHI: THE WAY THE BRANCHES GROW AND SPREAD.

Hisao Iwashimizu

IRONWARE ARTIST

Ironware artist Hisao Iwashimizu was born in 1964 in Morioka City. After graduating from the university, he began working for an environmental design company. He received the Design Plus award at the 1998 Ambiente international consumer goods fair and has received numerous awards in Japan, among them the Japan Craft Exhibition prize. The Museum of Modern Art in New York City showed his work in 2000. His work currently appears in one-man shows throughout Japan.

The first time I saw Iwashimizu's name in print was in the early 1990s. Then one day I was at a department store where there was an exhibition of Iwashimizu's work. Even though we were not acquainted with each other, we had the extraordinary experience of somehow knowing each other without being introduced: "You are Mr. Iwashimizu, right?" and "You're Kobayashi, aren't you!" At the time, we were both working for companies and had spoken on the phone to each other a number of times, but that was the first occasion when we'd met face to face. It was a great surprise to have run into each other like that in a huge crowd of strangers. Not long after that, when I had just started out on my own, it was Iwashimizu who came to keep me company at a marketing event at a candle company, and we began to develop a warm friendship.

Iron is an element that recalls the past; it is a material that returns to the earth after passing through eternities of time. Because of its composition, it changes color and even shape as it rusts. In terms of the Japanese aesthetic qualities of wabi and sabi, iron is what gives sabi—which is, in fact, the Japanese word for rust. It fuses the worlds of bonsai and Japanese candles, so it makes sense to have them come together. Iwashimizu goes so far as to say that in an austere space where color is used sparely, the tones introduced by bonsai are absolutely indispensable, and in fact we have since then worked together on a number of collaborative exhibitions.

The charmingly named tamago no ko (egg child) teapot for which Iwashimizu was awarded a design prize in Germany has a contemporary form and is the first piece that really demonstrated to me the softness of iron. This teapot has become Iwashimizu's trademark—and apparently the first person to purchase the teapot with the maple lid was me. Iwashimizu lives a busy life these days, commuting between his home in Yokohama and his studio in Mizusawa, but when he's back home, we have made it our custom to share a drink together. I look forward to it every time.

Opposite page: Tea prepared in the tamago no ko (egg child) teapot tastes extra good.

Ahiru no ko (duck's child), one in his series of teapots and sake holders, features Iwashimizu's original finish with its smooth exterior texture. He designed the cloth it rests on, too.

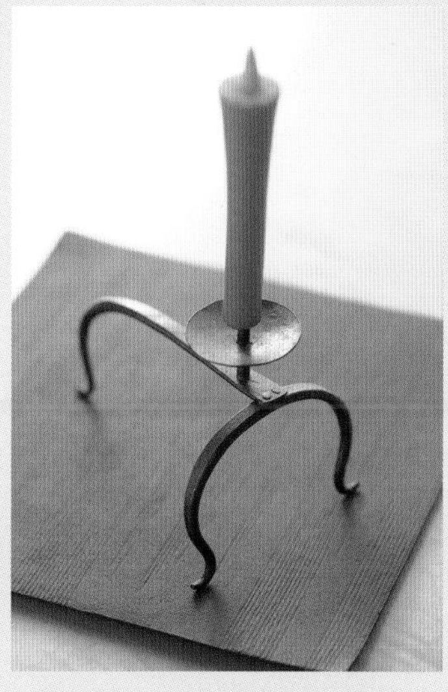

I'm especially fond of how the curved legs of this candleholder by Iwashimizu play into the design.

When Iwashimizu visits the shop, we talk like brothers about what's going on in our lives and laugh our heads off.

Iwashimizu's portfolio illustrates how the candleholder on the right-hand page was inspired by the intense rigidity of a cross he saw on a church.

Iwashimizu designed this candlestick with base and pole to showcase the rust on the iron. Bonsai and Japanese candles have a natural affinity and pair well with a modern interior space.

MOSS AND TREES

By adding to moss the strong personality of trees with their trunks and branches, you can create landscapes of great grandeur. With trees, you can enjoy the change of seasons and feel that nature is indeed close at hand.

A white container with brilliant green moss and tree

KESHIKI 6

MINIMALIST STYLE

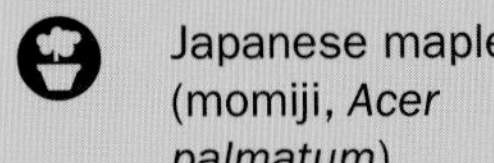

- Japanese maple (momiji, *Acer palmatum*)
- Japanese mountain moss (yamagoke)

- 2½ inches in diameter by 1¼ inches tall

1 Secure mesh over the drainage hole and add enough coarse-grain Fuji sand to cover the mesh. Then add enough potting mixture to cover this subsoil.

2 Remove the maple from its nursery pot and clean the soil from the surface and roots with tweezers. Use the tip of the tweezers to flick the soil away.

This small bit of the nature you might glimpse in a nearby park, captured in a clean white container, begs to be held in your hand and relished with lengthy gazes.

3 Decide where to place the maple. Position it so that the branches extend toward the interior and the plant is closer to the rim of the container than to the center.

FUTOKORO EDA: AN INNER BRANCH IN THE SHADOW OF A LARGER BRANCH.

4 After positioning it, hold the plant steady with your hand and add potting mixture. Use a chopstick to poke and tamp down the soil so there are no air pockets.

5 Use the plant mister to dampen the soil while tamping down and flattening it with the spatula. Let the water penetrate well into the soil.

6 Take a piece of moss slightly larger than the mouth of the container and use your fingers to pinch away old moss from the underside.

7 Spread the moss on the soil. Make a slit in the moss and fit it around the tree trunk, then use a chopstick to nudge the moss away from the edge and push it toward the center. Use different types of moss to create an expressive landscape.

8 Fill gaps with fine-grain Fuji sand as a decorative topdressing. Turn the pot slowly as you carefully pour in the sand.

9 Use the plant mister to dampen the moss and then tidying up the whole thing with your fingertips. Finish by watering enough for water to drain out the bottom.

DIFFERENT VARIETIES OF TREES

The two main types of trees are deciduous, which lose their leaves in autumn and winter, and evergreen, which keep their foliage all year long. The leaves of deciduous trees generally change color from green to yellow or red and vividly impart a sense of the season. It is also very satisfying to see the bare form of the tree after the leaves have fallen and then to watch buds form in the spring. As for evergreens, the vast variety of foliage forms and tree shapes offers something for everyone.
Be sure to select what appeals to you most.

On the right is tall stewartia (hime shara, *Stewartia monadelpha*) after leaf-fall. Other deciduous trees for landscape bonsai include Japanese maple (momiji, *Acer palmatum*), spike winter hazel (tosamizuki, *Corylopsis spicata*), and Japanese hornbeam (soro, *Carpinus japonica*). On the left is Japanese white pine (goyomatsu, *Pinus parviflora*). Other evergreens for bonsai include Japanese cypress (hinoki, *Chamaecyparis obtusa*), Japanese black pine (kuromatsu, *Pinus thunbergii*), and Japanese andromeda (asebi, *Pieris japonica*).

KESHIKI 7

The imposing beauty of a tall cypress

This simple tree has true presence. When placed on a staircase, it towers over the serene interior of a home and makes climbing the stairs a lot more fun.

EURO STYLE

Japanese cypress (hinoki, *Chamaecyparis obtusa*)

Japanese mountain moss (yamagoke)

5 inches in diameter by 4 inches tall

1 Secure mesh over the drainage hole and add enough coarse-grain Fuji sand to cover the mesh. Then add potting mixture so that the pot is a third full.

2 Remove the cypress from its nursery pot and clean away soil with tweezers. Be extra careful not to injure the roots.

3 Place the cypress in the pot and add soil so that the base of the roots is at the same level as the rim of the pot. Hold the tree steady with your hand so that its position does not change.

4 Use a chopstick to poke and tamp down the soil while adding more to the pot. Continue to hold the tree with your other hand until it is securely in place.

5 Use the plant mister to dampen the soil while tamping down and flattening it with the spatula. Let the water penetrate well into the soil.

6 Take a piece of moss slightly larger than the mouth of the container and use your fingers to pinch away old moss from the underside. Cut the clump of moss halfway down the center to fit around the base of the tree. Add little pieces of moss to create a hilly landscape.

7 Press down the moss with your hand and use a chopstick to push any moss that hangs over the side into the interior.

8 Fill gaps with fine-grain Fuji sand as a decorative topdressing. Turn the pot slowly as you carefully pour in the sand.

9 Use the plant mister to dampen the moss while smoothing the sand with the spatula. Finish by watering enough for water to drain out the bottom.

SELECTING TREES

To select a tree for your keshiki bonsai, first look at the general appearance of the trunk, branches, and leaves and choose a plant that looks strong and vigorous. Make sure that the leaves show no signs of insect bites or disease and that there are not a lot of fallen, withered leaves on the soil of the pot. (A weak tree will shed leaves in order to protect itself, so fallen leaves are a sign that the plant is not healthy.) Once you have determined that the tree is healthy, observe the form of the tree. Each tree has its own special personality, whether its form is upright or has many curves. Even trees of the same species present different branch formations. Choose the one that appeals to your taste.

On the right, a curved trunk lends character to a black pine. On the left, a Japanese cypress stands straight up.

The same type of tree can come in many shapes. Select what most appeals to you.

KESHIKI 8

Gracefully bending branches, a classic bonsai motif

JAPANESE STYLE

Japanese red pine (akamatsu, *Pinus densiflora*)

Japanese mountain moss (yamagoke)

5 inches in diameter by 4 inches tall

1 Secure mesh over the drainage hole and add enough coarse-grain Fuji sand to cover the mesh. Then add potting mixture so that the pot is a third full.

2 Use tweezers to remove dried-out, brown pine needles from the branches. The finished bonsai would look bedraggled if withered needles were left on the branch.

Planting only after the old and brown leaves have been cleaned off assures that the viewer will fully appreciate the texture and shape of the trunk and branches.

3 Remove the seedling from its nursery pot and clean away soil from the surface and roots with tweezers. Be extra careful not to injure the roots when untangling ones that have gotten twisted at the bottom of the pot.

4 Once you have removed enough soil so that the lower roots are exposed, cut off excess root length with scissors, being careful not to touch the roots. Heat from your body can damage the roots.

HA-GARI: LITERALLY, "DEFOLIATION"—CUTTING OFF ALL LEAVES AND LEAVING ONLY THE LEAF STALK, A PROCEDURE DONE IN LATE SPRING OR EARLY SUMMER.

5 Decide where to place the plant. The branches will extend to the right, so position it toward the back on the left. Find a position that appears balanced, paying close attention to the way the plant leans and the branch style (eda buri).

6 Use a chopstick to poke and tamp while adding soil to the pot. Continue to hold the tree with your other hand until it is securely in place.

7 Use the plant mister to dampen the soil while tamping it down and flattening it with the spatula. Let the water penetrate well into the soil.

8 Take a piece of moss slightly larger than the mouth of the container and use your fingers to pinch away old moss from the underside. Cut a slit halfway through the center and slide over the base of the plant so that the moss fits around it snugly. Then use the chopstick to push the moss on the edge firmly inside the ontainer.

9 Fill gaps with fine-grain Fuji sand as a decorative topdressing. Turn the pot slowly as you carefully pour in the sand.

10 Use the plant mister to dampen the moss while smoothing the sand with the spatula. Finish by watering enough for water to drain out the bottom.

MASTERING THE ART OF PRUNING LEAVES

Pruning bonsai is an art, so first we'll focus on a simple way for beginners to improve the look of the foliage. This procedure brings an orderly appearance to the leaves so that the bonsai is neat and pleasing to the eye.

Coralberry (manryo, *Ardisia crenata*) before and after tidying

BEFORE

AFTER

Pull yellowed leaves down before pulling off.

Thin out leaves below the berries to make the fruit stand out better.

CONTINUED

HAMONO: ORNAMENTALS BEARING LEAVES OF PARTICULAR VISUAL INTEREST.

HANAMONO: FLOWERING TREES, ESPECIALLY THOSE THAT BEAR FLOWERS EMBLEMATIC OF THE SEASON.

Chinese juniper (shinpaku, *Juniperus chinensis*) before and after tidying

BEFORE

AFTER

Pull off spiky new buds by pinching them between your fingers.

Remove enough buds to achieve a rounded profile for each branch.

Japanese black pine (kuromatsu, *Pinus thunbergii*) before and after tidying

BEFORE

AFTER

To promote nutrition reaching the strong needles and to make the beauty of the branches stand out, use scissors to cut away excess foliage.

KESHIKI 9

A grove of trees on
a hill of moss
in a silver bowl

Griffith's ash, a natural air purifier, creates the feeling of a miniature woods on top of a hill of moss in this keshiki bonsai. Just a single planter fills the room with comfort.

MINIMALIST STYLE

 Griffith's ash (shima-toneriko, *Fraxinus griffithii*)

 Japanese mountain moss (yamagoke)

 2¾ inches by 2¾ inches by 3½ inches tall

1 Secure mesh over the drainage hole and add enough coarse-grain Fuji sand to cover the mesh. Then add potting mixture to hide the subsoil.

2 Remove the seedling from its nursery pot and clean away soil from the surface and roots with tweezers. Be extra careful not to injure the roots when untangling ones that have gotten twisted at the bottom of the pot.

3 Once you have removed enough soil so that the lower roots are exposed, cut off excess root length with scissors, being careful not to touch the roots. Heat from your body can damage the roots.

4 Place the plant in the center of the container and add soil. Since there are a number of similarly sized branches extending from the root base, centering the plant creates the impression of a grove of trees.

5 Use a chopstick to poke and tamp while adding soil to the pot. Continue to hold the tree with your other hand until it is securely in place.

6 Use the plant mister to dampen the soil while tamping down and flattening it with the spatula. Let the water penetrate well into the soil. To enhance the sense of a miniature woods, remove leaves from the lower part of the plant.

7 Pinch off old growth from the underside of a fairly thick clump of moss, which will be used to fashion a small hill. Be conservative when removing the old moss, since pinching out too much will detract from the effect of a softly rounded mound, leaving it too thin.

8 Divide the moss into several pieces and place them over the base of the plant. This will create the contours that give the landscape its natural look.

9 In the gaps, add Kurama sand as the decorative topdressing.

10 Use the plant mister to dampen the moss while smoothing the sand with the spatula. Finish by watering enough for water to drain out the bottom.

HARIGANE KAKE: APPLYING WIRE TO THE TRUNK OR BRANCHES IN ORDER TO STYLE OR TRAIN A PLANT.

KESHIKI 10

A tree on a knoll
in a tall,
narrow container

EURO STYLE

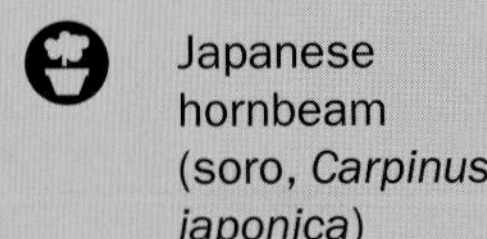

Japanese hornbeam (soro, *Carpinus japonica*)

Japanese mountain moss (yamagoke)

2½ inches in diameter by 3¼ inches tall

1 Thread aluminum wire through a piece of mesh placed in the bottom of the planter and pull the ends of the wire through the drainage hole, securing by bending the ends across the bottom.

2 Add enough coarse-grain Fuji sand to fill the container a third full. For containers without much height, the aim is to add enough subsoil to cover the mesh. In this case, however, the container is tall, which calls for more subsoil.

There is great charm to the lithely twisting branches stretching out to the side. The tiny leaves can't help but evoke a tender response.

3 Add enough potting mixture to cover the Fuji sand.

4 Remove the hornbeam from its nursery pot. It will come out more easily if you hold the base of the plant and then press the base of the pot.

5 Use a chopstick to clean away soil from the surface and roots. You can use tweezers if you prefer, but since the roots are short and not twisted, a chopstick works fine.

HEIKO EDA: BRANCHES THAT SPROUT PARALLEL TO EACH OTHER FROM AROUND THE SAME PLACE ON THE TRUNK.

6 Observe which way the tree is bending or inclining and position it in the container so that it appears balanced. Once you have decided on the position, hold the base of the plant between your fingers so that it will stay in place and add potting mixture.

7 Use a chopstick to poke at the soil and fill in gaps.

8 Use the plant mister to dampen the soil while tamping it down and flattening it with the spatula. Soak the soil uniformly.

9 Pinch off old growth from the back of a clump of moss, make a slit, and place the moss around the base of the plant.

10 Push the moss overhanging the sides of the container back inside with the chopstick. Press on the moss with your fingers to secure it in place.

11 In the gaps, add Kurama sand as the decorative topdressing, pouring it in slowly as you turn the container.

12 Use the plant mister to dampen the moss while smoothing the sand with the spatula. Finish by watering enough for water to drain out the bottom.

KESHIKI 11

Berries and leaves in a lush meadow

A mini bonsai with violet berries and green leaves, stylishly growing in a glass container, conjures all the pleasures of the four seasons. To show off the branches to their most beautiful effect, we trim the undersides, bringing focus to the form.

RUSTIC STYLE

Japanese beautyberry (murasaki shikibu, *Callicarpa japonica*)

Japanese mountain moss (yamagoke)

5 inches in diameter by 2¾ inches tall

1 Thread aluminum wire through a piece of mesh placed in the bottom of the planter and pull the ends of the wire through the drainage hole, securing by bending the ends across the bottom.

2 Add enough coarse-grain Fuji sand to hide the mesh.

3 Add enough potting mixture to cover the Fuji sand.

4 Before removing the seedling from its nursery pot, carefully remove any weeds that are growing on the surface of the soil, using tweezers to clear away the unwanted growth.

5 Remove the seedling from the pot and then scrape off moss from the surface with the tweezers. Moss can be a hiding place for insects, so it's a good idea to clear it away even if it looks clean.

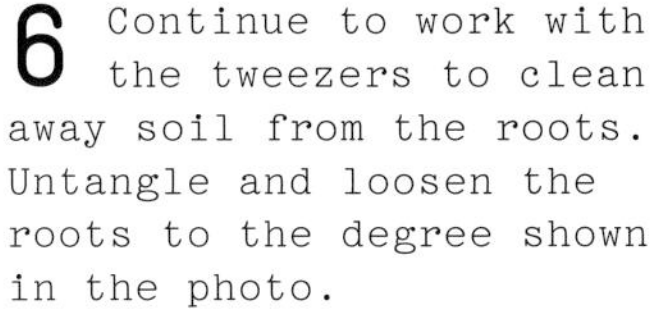

6 Continue to work with the tweezers to clean away soil from the roots. Untangle and loosen the roots to the degree shown in the photo.

7 Place the seedling in the container and add soil. Hold the base of the plant firmly to keep it in place.

8 Use a chopstick to poke at the soil and fill in any space between the roots. You may need to add more soil as you work so that no gaps or air pockets remain.

9 Spread moss on the soil after pinching off old moss from the backs of the clumps. Build it up so that it is dense and luxuriant, pushing the moss away from the edges of the container and toward the center with the chopstick.

10 Keep adding moss little by little until you have created the landscape of a lush, green hill. Press firmly on the seams between the small clumps of moss to smooth the surface.

11 When the soil is covered with moss, cut old branches with bonsai scissors to style the plant into the shape you want. To finish, water generously so that it drains from the bottom.

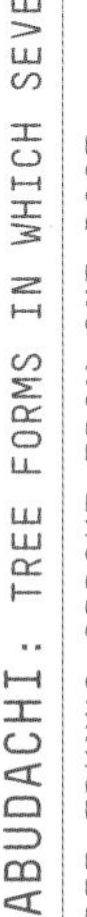

KABUDACHI: TREE FORMS IN WHICH SEVERAL TREE TRUNKS SPROUT FROM ONE ROOT.

Nobuo Hashiba

CONTEMPORARY ARTIST

The remarkable relief works by Hashiba have the texture of metal. Existing in its own realm somewhere between painting and sculpture, Hashiba's striking artwork is made of hardened layers of papier-mâché on canvas coated with metal powder, oxidized silver, or gold paint using a technique that produces an uneven surface. A characteristic of his pieces is the use of raised dots alluding to the elementary particles that form all matter on earth; each dot bears a fingerprint from the moment when it was formed out of papier-mâché. The inspiration comes from the time in the early 1980s when the artist was in France and saw the handprint of a prehistoric ancestor in the Lascaux caves. Hashiba says he was "heart struck" to find this trace of the person who painted the cave; ever since, he has worked at leaving his own personal mark on the pieces he makes.

Born 1950 in Tokyo, Hashiba holds solo shows and participates in group exhibitions all over Japan. He has received numerous commissions from major corporations, hotels, and traditional inns where his artwork is on display. Internationally, he has shown work in group shows in France and New York, and at the Shanghai Art Fair. He began collaborating with flower artist Toshiro Kawase in 1996.

I first met Hashiba in 2004 at a Tokyo department store that was holding an exhibition called "thinking about contemporary floors." I was participating in a neighboring exhibition on the theme of "thinking about contemporary gardens." While looking at Hashiba's "colored reliefs" I felt I was being pulled into the world of wabi-sabi where the aesthetic ideal is weathered, to look as though made through the forces of nature. His feeling for the imperfect, for a rough refinement that is at once simple and

This keshiki bonsai shines in solitary refinement in Hashiba's studio beside one of his paintings. The lines of the plant seem to trace the features of a face.

A work by Hashiba placed above a Korean Joseon dynasty chest and a carefully prepared bonsai forms a study in contrasts.

Sculptures and objets d'art are placed for impact on an open shelf; there's a fantastic synergy between the gorgeous Asian lily and the piece with the face of the Paekche bodhisattva (a Korean religious sculpture).

Four Chinese deities complement a piece by Hashiba, "Untitled." Subdued but complex, his artwork lends itself to broad-ranging styles, particularly those inflected with contemplative beauty.

profound, struck me as being completely in sync with the world of bonsai that I was creating.

Hashiba's style, which seeks forms that aren't just historical but that respond to the modern world, derives from exactly the world that I am striving to express. Hashiba tells me that my work is about the use of space, precisely what I feel his work punctuates. The interaction of keshiki bonsai with a painting by Hashiba on the wall and furniture ravaged by the nicks and scratches of history creates a mood that touches a place deep inside; for me, the experience is a sense of tranquility both boundless and deep. While his and my work inhabit their independent spheres, Hashiba's art and keshiki bonsai have a synergy that plays off their unexpected convergence. I look forward to the chance for more collaborations in the future.

Here I am chatting with the ever sociable and stylish Hashiba. Despite his being busy getting ready for his next exhibition, time flies by as we talk, one subject leading to the next.

MOSS, TREES, PERENN

AND

IALS

At last, we are ready for the challenge of bringing perennials into the picture. This broad grouping encompasses flowers and foliage, grasses and ground covers, a theatrical troupe with its stars and supporting actors. Perennials of all varieties lend graceful counterbalance to potted arrangements and impart a special charm that adds to the fullness of nature within a container.

A wild mountain landscape you loved as a child

KESHIKI 12

RUSTIC STYLE

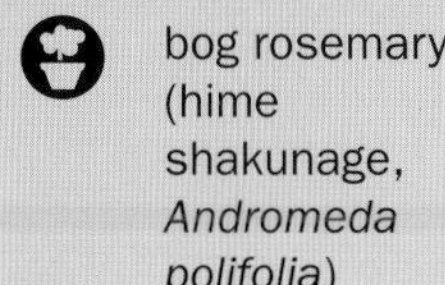

- bog rosemary (hime shakunage, *Andromeda polifolia*)
- multiflora rose (noibara, *Rosa multiflora*)
- Japanese mountain moss (yamagoke)

2¾ inches by 2¾ inches by 3½ inches tall

A multiflora rose with thorns removed from the base of the plant is accompanied by undergrowth of bog rosemary to create the sense of a wooded mountainside.

1 Secure drainage mesh in the bottom of the container and add enough coarse-grain Fuji sand to hide the mesh. Next, add potting mixture until the container is about a third full.

2 Remove the multiflora rose from its nursery pot and clean away soil from the surface and roots with tweezers. Snip off the thorns near the base of the plant.

3 Use the tweezers to untwist the roots while at the same time clearing away soil until the plant looks like the photo.

KAN NUKI EDA: BRANCHES THAT EMERGE FROM THE SAME POINT ON THE TRUNK AND BRANCH OUT TO THE LEFT AND RIGHT; LITERALLY, "BOLT BRANCHES," SO CALLED BECAUSE THEY RESEMBLE THE BOLT THAT KEEPS A DOOR OR GATE SHUT.

4 Remove the bog rosemary from its nursery pot. Wash the roots by pouring water into a bowl and immersing the roots. Clean away the dirt with your fingertips while untangling the roots.

5 Place the bog rosemary and the multiflora rose in the container, position them, and add soil. Use a chopstick to poke the soil and add more as needed to fill in the gaps.

6 Fill the container with soil up to about 1/4 inch from the rim. Use the plant mister to dampen the soil while flattening it with the spatula.

7 Pinch off old growth from the back of a clump of moss and press the moss into place. Use the chopstick to push the moss into an even shape.

8 In the spaces between the plants, add coarse-grain Fuji sand as a decorative topdressing. Spray with water while smoothing the surface with the spatula, and finish by watering.

KESHIKI 13

Grasses sprouting from a jar-shaped pot

Grasses can seem to merge with the pot they grow in. Consider the overall form produced by the plant and its container and think of the two as one design element, then enjoy the visual interest of their combined contours. Placed on a bookshelf, the solid form instills a sense of harmony.

MINIMALIST STYLE

dwarf sweet flag (hime sekisho, *Acorus gramineus*)

Japanese mountain moss (yamagoke)

3¼ inches outer diameter and 1½ inches inner diameter by 2½ inches tall

1 Secure drainage mesh in the bottom of the pot and fill with coarse-grain Fuji sand until the mesh is no longer visible. Then add potting mixture so that the pot is a third full.

2 Wash the roots of the grass by pouring water into a bowl and immersing the roots. Clean the dirt away gently with your fingertips.

3 Place the grass in the pot and use a chopstick to tuck the roots into the pot.

4 Hold the plant in place with your hand to keep it from moving as you add more soil.

5 Use the chopstick to pack the soil into gaps. Because of the shape of the container, it's important to fill the entire interior with soil. The gentle pressure from the chopstick will help ensure that no air pockets remain inside.

6 Use the plant mister to dampen the soil while smoothing it with the spatula; spread the moss on top after first removing old growth from the back.

7 Push moss away from the edge of the container with the chopstick and finish by watering.

KESHIKI 14

This strikingly vertical arrangement in a large bowl combines three types of plants found in woodsy waterside landscapes. Bear in mind that root washing is recommended for grasses with long, delicate stalks.

The bold lines of horsetails in a waterside landscape

JAPANESE STYLE

 horsetail (*Equisetum hyemale*)

 azure bluet (hinaso, *Houstonia caerulea*)

 goldenthread (baika-oren, *Coptis quinquefolia*)

 Japanese mountain moss (yamagoke)

 14 inches in diameter by 4 inches tall

1 Secure drainage mesh in the bottom of the container and add enough coarse-grain Fuji sand to hide the mesh. Next, add potting mixture so that the container is about a third full.

2 Remove the horsetails from the nursery pot and clean away soil from the roots with tweezers. Work slowly, bit by bit, untangling the roots to clean away the soil lodged inside.

3 Remove the bluets from the nursery pot and place in a bowl of water to wash the roots with your fingers.

4 Place the plants on a dishtowel and fold it over the roots to absorb excess water. Do the same for the goldenthread.

5 Arrange the plants in the container, positioning them to achieve balance. Divide the horsetails into large, medium, and small stalks and place the large ones in front, the medium ones toward the back on the right, and the small ones toward the back on the left.

6 Fill the container with soil up to about 1/2 inch from the rim and tamp it down lightly so that the plants are secured in place. Poke the soil with the chopstick and add more soil to the gaps.

7 Use the plant mister to dampen the soil while smoothing it with the spatula, making sure that the water penetrates thoroughly.

8 Remove old growth from the back of the moss and then use the chopstick to hold the plants back as you place the moss. Aim for uneven contours, forming small hillocks of moss between the plants.

9 Add fine-grain Fuji sand as a decorative topdressing. You will want to cover all the potting mixture with the sand, so pour it in carefully.

10 Use the plant mister to dampen the sand while smoothing it with the spatula; apply enough moisture to soak the soil. Finish by watering thoroughly.

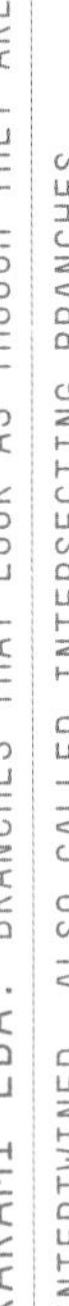

KESHIKI 15

A densely overgrown forest in a sleekly modern bowl

A chic container creates an unexpected counter-balance to dense plantings. This arrangement is enhanced by planting a flowering plant so that it appears to be sprouting from the base of the heavenly bamboo. Once this is established and growing well, reduce watering.

MINIMALIST STYLE

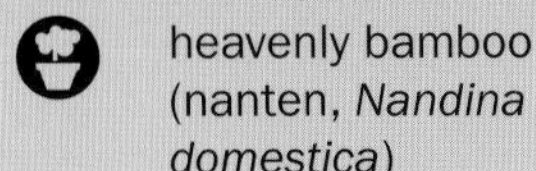

- heavenly bamboo (nanten, *Nandina domestica*)
- cremanthodium (hime-tsuwabuki, *Cremanthodium campanulatum*)
- Japanese mountain moss (yamagoke)

- 7 inches in diameter by 2¾ inches tall

1 Secure drainage mesh in the bottom of the container and add enough coarse-grain Fuji sand to hide the mesh. Next, add potting mixture so that the container is about a third full.

2 Remove the heavenly bamboo from the nursery pot and clean away soil from the surface and roots with tweezers.

3 Once you have removed most of the soil, cut off the excess root length with scissors.

4 Remove the cremanthodium from the nursery pot and wash the roots by placing them in a bowl of water and gently removing soil with your fingertips.

5 To make it appear that the cremanthodium is budding from the base of the heavenly bamboo, line up the two seedlings and place them in the container together. Fill with potting soil.

6 Use a chopstick to poke at the soil, then fill in gaps with additional soil as you hold onto the leaves to keep the plants from moving. Use a plant mister to dampen the surface and then smooth with the spatula. Soak with water.

7 Spread the moss on top after removing old growth from the back. Create the landscape by piecing together small bits of moss as you press the edges of the individual clumps into the soil using the chopstick.

KAWA HAGI: REMOVING A PORTION OF BARK FROM THE TRUNK OR BRANCHES.

KENGAI: A TREE PROFILE IN WHICH MOST OF THE TRUNK DRAPES BELOW THE ROOTS.

8 Fill in gaps between the plants by adding fine-grain Fuji sand as a decorative topdressing.

9 Use the plant mister to dampen the sand while smoothing with the spatula. Finish by watering.

SELECTING PERENNIALS

One of the basic criteria for selecting a plant is that the entire plant be healthy and strong. Take the seedling in your hand and check that the stems are firm. Those that have taken root well will have buds or show a surge of new growth and good color.

Plants that have many buds. An abundance of buds is proof that the plant is healthy. This is a sign that you can anticipate a continuous display of flowers blossoming after the seedling is planted.

Plants with no withered leaves. Be sure to check the interior of the plant, which may be hidden by leaves. Move the leaves aside by hand; if there are no dead leaves, the plant can be considered healthy.

Plants with flower buds at the base. A very good sign of vigor is flower buds tinged with color appearing at the base of the plant. These show that the plant is healthy and can be used with confidence.

KESHIKI 16

A striking vertical planting in a brass bowl

Bonsai planted in a brass bowl creates a sharp, masculine atmosphere. Remove old leaves from Kuma bamboo grass for a neat, clear-cut shape. This not only improves the flow of air through the plant but also creates a striking appearance.

JAPANESE STYLE

- coralberry (hyakuryo, *Ardisia crispa*; or manryo, *Ardisia crenata*)
- Kuma bamboo grass (koguma-zasa, *Sasa veitchii*)
- Japanese mountain moss (yamagoke)

- 2½ inches in diameter by 2¾ inches tall

1 Secure drainage mesh in the bottom of the container and add enough coarse-grain Fuji sand to hide the mesh. Next, add potting mixture so that the container is about a third full.

2 Use tweezers to clean away dirt from the surface and roots of the coralberry. Place the Kuma bamboo grass in a bowl of water for root washing and untangling.

3 After washing the soil off the bamboo grass roots, cut the main root. What look like thin whiskers are the secondary roots; the thicker strand is the main root.

4 Protect the roots in keto peat soil after cutting. Bundle small sections of roots together and cover them all in the peat soil as though wrapping them in a mud pack.

5 Place the coralberry in the container and then add the bamboo grass with its roots still wrapped in peat soil. Fill the container with potting soil, using a chopstick to tamp the soil down and remove air pockets.

6 Use the plant mister to dampen the surface and then smooth with the spatula. Soak with water to provide a receptive surface where the moss can establish easily.

7 Remove old growth from the back of the moss and then spread it over the surface, mounding it to form a rounded hill. Press the edges toward the center using the chopstick.

KESHIKI 17

Griffith's ash yields numerous stalks once the roots are washed and the plant divided. Planting dwarf sweet flag between the wispy stems of the ash makes a nice arrangement.

The feeling of wind in the branches on a tabletop

EURO STYLE

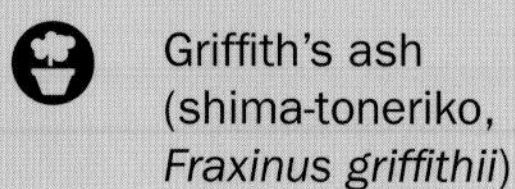

- Griffith's ash (shima-toneriko, *Fraxinus griffithii*)
- dwarf sweet flag (hime sekisho, *Acorus gramineus*)
- Japanese mountain moss (yamagoke)

- 2¾ inches in diameter by 2 inches tall

1 Secure drainage mesh in the bottom of the container and add enough coarse-grain Fuji sand to hide the mesh. Next, add potting mixture so that the container is about a third full.

2 Remove the ash from the nursery pot and clean away soil from the surface and roots with tweezers. Untangle the roots.

3 Once you have removed a fair amount of soil, break off just the section you want to use and plant the rest in another container. When dividing the roots, refrain from pulling with too much force.

4 Remove the grass from the nursery pot and wash the roots by placing them in a bowl of water and gently removing as much soil as you can with your fingertips.

5 Take two stalks of ash and place them to either side of the grass. Slip the arrangement into the container and consider the composition: observe how the branches spread and reposition if needed to create a balanced profile.

6 Add potting soil and tamp down with a chopstick to remove air pockets. Use the plant mister to dampen the surface while smoothing with the spatula.

7 Remove old growth from the back of the clump of moss and form the landscape by covering the exposed soil with the moss.

TYPES OF PERENNIALS

Perennials can be categorized into two groups: those with interesting foliage and those that bear flowers or fruit. Among these, there are a variety of growth patterns with some stretching up vertically, some that spread horizontally, and some that grow in a fanlike configuration. Bear these differences in mind when making your selection, and choose the type that best suits the shape and style you are after.

Perennials that bear flowers or berries:
1. Japanese chrysanthemum (kangiku, *Chrysanthemum indicum*) has small, brilliant-hued flowers and nice, full volume.
2. Japanese ardisia (yabukoji, *Ardisia japonica*) displays berries with a fresh red color.
3. Azure bluets (hinaso, *Houstonia caerulea*) bear tiny flowers, full of charm.

Perennials with fanciful leaf forms:
1. The low, striped Kuma bamboo grass (koguma-zasa, *Sasa veitchii*) has thin leaves with straight edges.
2. The wildflower goldenthread (baika-oren, *Coptis quinquefolia*) has leaves with a notched pattern.
3. Round-leaved cyclamen *(Cyclamen coum)* sends out rounded leaves displaying a pattern faintly traced in silver.
4. Horsetail (tokusa, *Equisetum hyemale*) grows straight up.
5. Mondo grass (*Ophiopogon japonicus* 'Hakuryu') has long, slender leaves with white markings.

8 Press the edges of the moss toward the center of the container using the chopstick. When the entire surface is covered with moss, finish by watering.

KETO: A CLAYEY, SOFT, TUNDRALIKE SOIL WITH DEEP DARK BROWN COLOR.

KESHIKI 18

Spreading branches in a full-bodied container

JAPANESE STYLE

- African bush daisy (ma-gareto kosumosu, *Euryops* species)
- bog rosemary (hime shakun-age, *Andromeda polifolia*)
- Japanese mountain moss (yamagoke)

- 8 inches in diameter by 2½ inches tall

1 Secure drainage mesh in the bottom of the container and add enough coarse-grain Fuji sand to hide the mesh. Next, add potting mixture so that the container is about a third full.

2 Remove the African bush daisy from the nursery pot and clean away soil from the surface and roots with tweezers. Work patiently, slowly, and carefully.

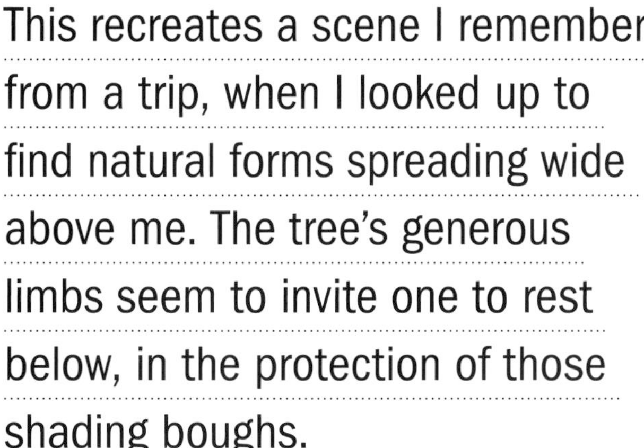

This recreates a scene I remember from a trip, when I looked up to find natural forms spreading wide above me. The tree's generous limbs seem to invite one to rest below, in the protection of those shading boughs.

3 Remove three bog rosemary seedlings from their nursery pots and wash the roots in a bowl of water by immersing them and gently cleaning away the soil with your fingertips.

KIRIKOMI: SUBSTANTIAL PRUNING OF BRANCHES OR TRUNKS DONE BY MAKING DEEP OR BIG CUTS.

4 Place the African bush daisy and the bog rosemary seedlings in the container and decide how to position them. Consider how the branches are growing and the configuration of leaves, and arrange the plants to achieve balance.

5 Add soil and use a chopstick to tamp down and remove air pockets. While working, hold the plants with your hand to keep them in place. Filling the gaps with more soil will further stabilize the plants.

6 Use the plant mister to dampen the soil, and smooth it with the spatula, making sure the water penetrates thoroughly to create a moist base for the moss to spread.

7 Spread the moss. Form several dense mounds of moss to create a mountainous landscape. Use the chopstick to press the edges of the moss toward the center.

8 Add fine-grain Fuji sand around and between the plants as a decorative topdressing. Use the plant mister to dampen the sand while smoothing with the spatula. Finish by watering thoroughly.

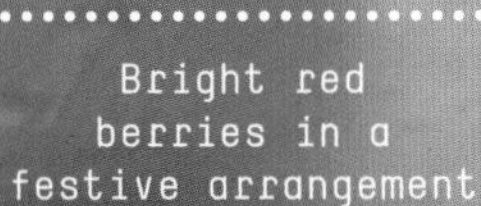

Bright red berries in a festive arrangement

KESHIKI 19

RUSTIC STYLE

 coralberry (hyakuryo, *Ardisia crispa*; or manryo, *Ardisia crenata*)

 heavenly bamboo (nanten, *Nandina domestica*)

 goldenthread (baika oren, *Coptis quinquefolia*)

 Japanese mountain moss (yamagoke)

 5 inches in diameter by 2¾ inches tall

The straight, slender stem and red berries of coralberry rise from a froth of red and green leaves in a shiny bowl. The heavenly bamboo should extend about halfway up the stalk of the coralberry.

1 Secure drainage mesh in the bottom of the container and add enough coarse-grain Fuji sand to hide the mesh. Next, add potting mixture so that the container is about a third full.

2 Remove the coralberry from its nursery pot and clean away soil from the surface and roots with tweezers.

3 Remove the heavenly bamboo from its nursery pot and clean away soil from the surface and roots with tweezers.

4 Remove the goldenthread from its nursery pot and wash the roots by placing them in a bowl of water and using your fingertips to remove soil.

5 Arrange the seedlings in the container, placing the coralberry first, then the heavenly bamboo, ending with the goldenthread. Create a dense planting that evokes a forest landscape.

6 Add soil and use a chopstick to tamp it down to remove air pockets. While working, hold the plants with your hand to keep them in place.

7 Use the plant mister to dampen the soil and then smooth it with the spatula, making sure that the water soaks in thoroughly.

8 Remove old growth from the back of the moss, cut slots in the clump, and place the pieces between the plants. Use the chopstick to press the edges of the moss toward the center. Finish by watering thoroughly.

KUITSUKI EDA: A SHORT BRANCH THICK WITH LEAVES GROWING DIRECTLY FROM THE TRUNK.

HOW TO DIVIDE PERENNIALS

If the potted seedling has plentiful foliage, remove enough soil so that you can see the roots. The plant is easy to divide if you cut the roots that connect two shoots. (If the roots are not connected, simply separate the shoots). It is easy to style a landscape by using the seedling pieces one by one or pairing two together.

1 Start with one seedling (in this photo, *Ophiopogon japonicus*) in a nursery pot.

2 Remove soil with tweezers until the roots are visible.

3 Cut the roots that join the shoots.

4 The seedling has been divided into nine new plants.

KESHIKI 20

A mini bonsai bewitching in its delicacy

EURO STYLE

- variegated Japanese andromeda (fu-iri asebi, *Pieris japonica* 'Variegata')
- variegated multiflora rose (fu-iri noibara, *Rosa multiflora* 'Variegata')
- Japanese mountain moss (yamagoke)

- 5 inches in diameter by 1½ inches tall

1 Secure the drainage mesh in the bottom of the container and add enough coarse-grain Fuji sand to hide the mesh. Then add potting mixture so that the Fuji sand is not visible.

Imagine an intimate afternoon tea made magical by the scaled-down focus of a living work of art. A trick to showing the clean lines of the Japanese andromeda is to tidy up the leaves so that the branches are plainly visible. Using variegated plants enhances the colorful brilliance.

2 Remove the andromeda from its nursery pot and clean away soil from the surface and roots with tweezers.

3 Trim the leaves from the andromeda: remove any leaves that cross the branches, and beyond that, remove enough so that the line of the stem is clearly defined.

4 Remove the multiflora rose from its nursery pot and likewise clean away soil from the surface and roots with tweezers.

5 Place the andromeda right-rear and then place the rose in front of that. Add soil and use a chopstick to tamp away air pockets.

6 Use the plant mister to dampen the soil, and smooth it with the spatula. Keep misting until the soil is soaked.

7 Spread the moss: remove old growth from the back, cut slots in the clump, and place it around the base of the plants. Use the chopstick to press the edges of the moss toward the center.

8 Add fine-grain Fuji sand as topdressing. Use the plant mister to dampen the sand while flattening with the spatula. Finish by watering.

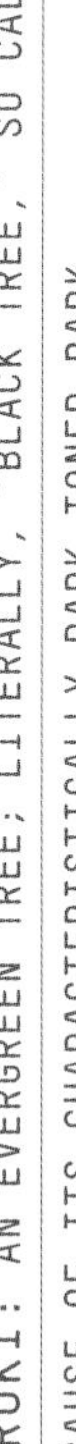

KESHIKI 21

A vigorous branch exuding strength

RUSTIC STYLE

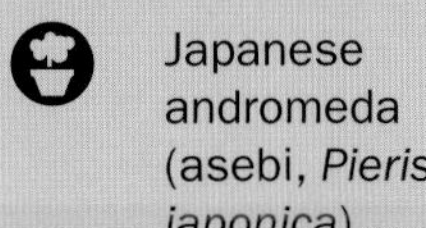

- Japanese andromeda (asebi, *Pieris japonica*)
- goldenthread (baika-oren, *Coptis quinquefolia*)
- Japanese mountain moss (yamagoke)

- 5½ inches in diameter by 4 inches tall

1 Secure drainage mesh in the bottom of the container and add enough coarse-grain Fuji sand to hide the mesh. Then add potting mixture so that the container is about a third full.

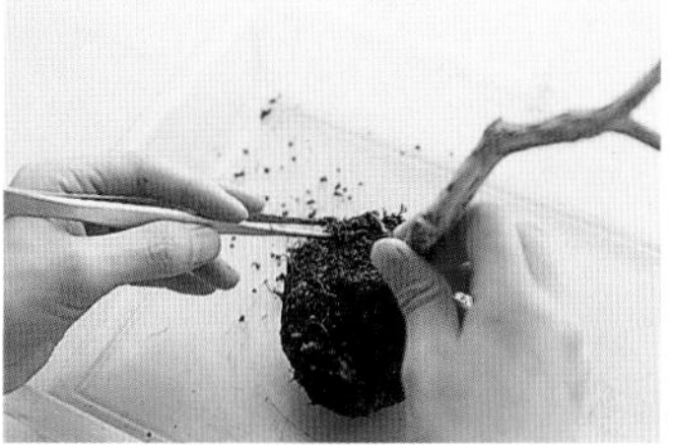

2 Remove the andromeda from its nursery pot and clean away soil from the surface and roots with tweezers.

3 Carefully remove brown, withered leaves from the andromeda one by one. This ensures that the finished arrangement will have a clean, healthy look.

This bonsai has presence—you can sense a powerful life spirit. Envision a tree growing from a cluster of green plants. Fill your room with natural drama that far outstrips the arrangement's footprint.

KUSA MONO: BONSAI MADE WITH WILD MOUNTAIN GRASSES.

KYOKUKAN: TREE TRUNKS THAT ARE TWISTED AND BENT.

4 Remove the goldenthread from its nursery pot and wash the roots in a bowl of water. Use your fingertips to gently clean away soil.

5 Place the andromeda right-rear and then place the goldenthread at its base. Add soil and use a chopstick to tamp away air pockets.

6 Use the plant mister to dampen the soil, and smooth it with the spatula. Soak the soil with water so that the moss can establish easily.

7 Remove old growth from the back of the moss and place clumps around the base of the plants, starting at the stems of the plants and working out from there. Placing a large mound of moss at the front of the arrangement gives the landscape depth, making the smaller forms in the back appear farther away.

8 Add fine-grain Fuji sand as topdressing to fill in the gaps. Use the plant mister to moisten the sand while flattening with the spatula. Finish by watering.

TIPS FOR COMBINING MOSS, TREES, AND PERENNIALS

When creating a landscape, you can use your imagination in a variety of ways to come up with the composition you like. For instance, you can recall actual scenes you have seen in nature and select plants that correspond, or you might be attracted to a particular plant and create your arrangement based on that. No matter what inspires you, here are a few pointers to help you achieve an effective landscape.

Envision the way a forest grows gradually out from a central cluster. Woods grow through thickets of grass and out the other side. Plant grass in dense mounds in the front of your arrangement and then position the tree beyond that, in the back. Grasses are especially compelling when planted in the front to give perspective to the composition.

Aim at recreating the way plants sprout from the bare surface of a hill. Walking along a path, you may notice animal tracks cutting a swath through the woods along the slopes. If you follow it, you will notice the woods seeming to spread out as you go deeper and deeper into the forest. Let moss serve as the hillside, and the space between the clumps of moss as the animal path, then use plants that mound thickly at the entrance to the woods, and trees for the woods extending out toward the back of the container. Freeze a frame from a mental film of memory recalling a hike through the hills, and use that as your starting point for recreating a woodland scene.

Imagine a grove of assorted trees in a woodland. Think of a stand of many trees in a woodland that is in full bloom. Bring to your bonsai the warmly remembered feeling from a landscape pulled from the mists of a fairytale or childhood memory. Form knolls of moss to deliver a sense of scale, and plant dainty perennials at the base of a tree to create a serene space.

MATA EDA: SMALL BRANCHES GROWING FROM THE SIDE OF THE MAIN BRANCH.

MEI: LITERALLY, "SIGNATURE"—THE NAME GIVEN TO A TREE.

Mito Yajima

CERAMICS ARTIST

Mito Yajima graduated from Musashino Junior College of Art and Design and now works as a professional artist after ten years of teaching ceramics. She mostly focuses on making tableware, flower vases, and other pieces of similar scale. Her work has been shown in craft exhibitions throughout Japan and won honorable mention at the Sapporo craft exhibition Geijutsu no Mori.

I first saw Yajima's work at an exhibition. Her ceramics struck me as being distinctive, conveying a whimsical personality with a modern edge. Somewhat later, unexpectedly, I met the artist at a department store exhibition, just as I was looking for a collaborator to work on a show I was planning for a department store in Kansai in western Japan. I knew right away that running into her was no accident: it was fate! She consented without hesitation as soon as I proposed the idea. That occasion prompted a friendship that's continued ever since.

Yajima's ceramics start with a layer of clay cut like a board and then formed into a shape using the slab-building method (tatara-zukuri), giving her work its sharp precision and geometric pattern. Her pieces speak to modern art with their sleek, uncluttered lines and weightless simplicity. Used as containers for keshiki bonsai, Yajima's ceramics add an extra shimmer to an interior, creating the perfect setting for an appreciation of modern art.

Moreover, the teacups that Yajima makes are not just for drinking tea—at the base of the cup is a small clay bell that makes a little rattle when you touch it. These unique objects call out to be used for drinking, for admiring, and for enjoying their sound, conveying some of Yajima's good humor and irrepressible laughter.

Her house, where she has her studio, conveys an atmosphere of calm with its pared-down modern Japanese style. Taking advantage of my visit there to interview her, I tried my hand at the potter's wheel. While enjoying the relaxed pleasure of her company, enveloped in the scent of the clay, I became completely seduced by the charm of ceramics.

Here I am, trying my hand at it. "I did it!" Her kind response: "Quite a good arm you've got there!" I was on Cloud Nine.

Stark angles create a beguiling contrast for keshiki bonsai. Horsetails, a favorite of Yajima's, in a keshiki bonsai using one of her pots create a contemporary living sculpture of quiet elegance.

Most of her pieces are slab-built, giving them the clean refinement of modern art.

These teacups with clay bells inside have become trademarks of Yajima's work. They make a sound when you hold them in your hand.

Yajima's gallery doubles as her living space. We're never at a loss for conversation topics, as our talk turns from ceramics to music and recollections of our fathers.

MOSS, TREES, PERENNIALS, STONES

Adding stones to the landscape makes it that much more real, a step closer to the essence of nature. In a garden, a large stone might be used for crossing a stream or as a step; small ones might be used to suggest the presence of water. Many facets, many textures, many moods arise with the use of stones in keshiki bonsai.

IALS, AND

KESHIKI 22

A small
garden in a tin
container

RUSTIC STYLE

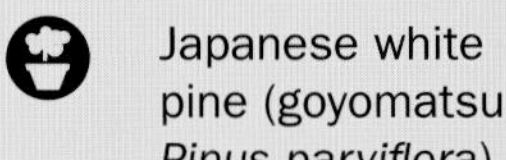

- Japanese white pine (goyomatsu, *Pinus parviflora*)
- Japanese mountain moss (yamagoke)

- 2½ inches in diameter by 1¾ inches tall

1 Secure drainage mesh in the bottom of the container and add enough coarse-grain Fuji sand to hide the mesh. Then add enough potting mixture to hide the Fuji sand.

2 Remove the pine from its nursery pot and clean away soil from the surface and roots with tweezers.

Simply by adding one stone, you can simulate the essence of a garden. Decorating the top of a weathered chest, the arrangement transforms the interior of the room with an evocative accent.

3 Place the pine and the stone in the container. To position the stone to best effect, first turn it so you can observe all its different surfaces and then position it on the soil so that it shows the side you decide is best. Imagine a garden and place the elements accordingly.

4 Hold the stone with your fingers so that it does not move as you add soil.

5 Use a chopstick to prod the soil and remove air pockets. Continue to hold the stone with your fingers so that it does not become dislodged.

METSUMI: PINCHING OFF STRONG NEW BUDS WHILE THEY ARE STILL SOFT AND BEFORE THEY START TO SPROUT.

6 Remove old growth from the back of the moss and press the clump to form a hill-like mound. Cut a slot into the moss so you can slip it around the base of the pine. Then use the chopstick to push the edges of the moss toward the center.

7 Fill in the bare spots with Kurama sand as a decorative topdressing. It is easiest to do this while turning the container.

8 Use the plant mister to dampen the sand while flattening it with the spatula. Finish by watering.

DIFFERENT VARIETIES OF STONES

In bonsai, stones are named according to their shapes. To make it easier for beginners, though, I've selected several stones that are used often to compose landscapes, and I will introduce them without these descriptors. When using stones in a small container, the smallest sizes can be used as topdressing that represents water, a river, or even the sea. Large stones, conversely, give the sense of boulders or stone steps. Coloration also varies from white to brown to black; experiment with the shade to create the mood you are after. Remember that the color of stones changes when they are wet with water, altering the mood to bring another dimension to the bonsai.

Top row, from left: mikaho stones, kuroboku stones, broken stones, artificial stone.
Middle row: white granite, Nachiguro stones (small and medium), white Nachi stones.
Bottom row: yasazuna stones, medium-grain Fuji sand, fine-grain Kurama sand, fine-grain Fuji sand.

KESHIKI 23

An indoor prairie in an earth-toned container

The rounded lines of an earth-toned container bring the prairie indoors, enhanced by variegated plants and light-colored stones. Peat adds height while moss creates an undulating dimension. Pumice stones produce a sense of light and harmony.

MINIMALIST STYLE

variegated Mt. Fuji rockcress (fu-iri hatazao *Arabis serrata* 'Variegata')

Japanese mountain moss (yamagoke)

4 inches in diameter by 2½ inches tall

1 Secure drainage mesh in the bottom of the container and add enough coarse-grain Fuji sand to hide the mesh. Next, add potting mixture so that the container is about a third full.

2 Remove three bunches of rockcress from the nursery pot and clean away soil from the surface and roots with tweezers, being careful not to damage the roots. Arrange the seedlings in the container.

3 Hold up the leaves of one seedling at a time and add soil, using a chopstick to remove air pockets and tamp down the soil. As you do this, make fine adjustments in how the plants are arranged, taking into consideration the shape of the leaves and the way the plants are facing.

4 Cover the area around the plants with peat, forming raised areas and adding dimension to the overall arrangement. Raise the left side higher to give a staggered effect when the stone is set in place.

5 Set pumice stones into the peat soil one by one. It is easiest if you first outline the area and then fill it in with stones to form the arrangement.

6 After removing old growth from the back of the moss, place the moss on the side opposite the rocks. Use the chopstick to push the moss away from the edge.

7 Carefully pour Kurama sand in the spaces not filled by stones or moss, to serve as a decorative topdressing. Be sure not to get the sand onto the leaves of the plants or onto the moss.

8 Use the plant mister to dampen the sand while smoothing it with the spatula. Finish by watering.

PLACEMENT OF STONES

Adding stones to a keshiki bonsai arrangement heightens its sense of being a real landscape. Observe a stone closely, turning it to see how changing the angle presents a different aspect. Get an understanding of the stone's characteristics, and experiment by placing it with different sides showing to see how that affects the sense of its weight, strength, stability, intensity, or other attribute. A basic rule is always to use an odd number of stones if using more than one.

Use the rocks as cliffs. Place two fairly large rocks on the left, facing the same direction, and then place one smaller stone on the right. The steep taper of a rugged cliff becomes perceptible if you let the sharp part of the stone show above the ground.

Use the rocks as stepping stones. In this arrangement, the same stones are used, but they have been placed with their smooth, flat sides showing. The smallest stone is placed in the foreground, followed by the next largest and the very largest at the back, inviting the viewer to step into the scene as though walking on a garden path.

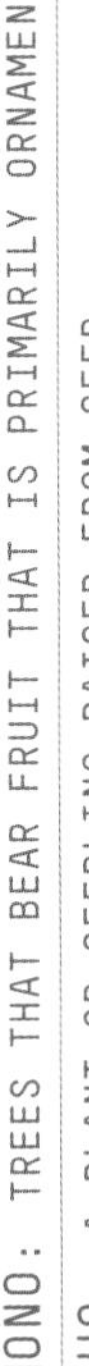

KESHIKI 24

A trickling stream where fireflies might appear

This arrangement of stones and moss suggests the clear trickle of a stream. The trunk of the black pine looks as if it were flowing from right to left. With all its needles pointing up, the tree appears strong and balances the composition.

JAPANESE STYLE

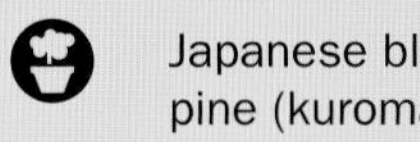
Japanese black pine (kuromatsu, *Pinus thunbergii*)

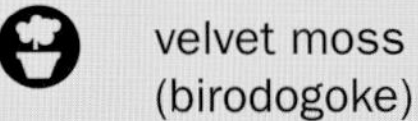
velvet moss (birodogoke)

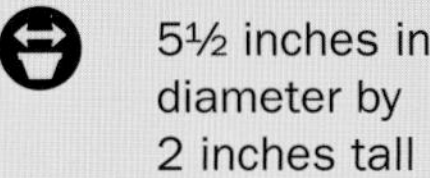
5½ inches in diameter by 2 inches tall

1 Secure drainage mesh in the bottom of the container and add enough coarse-grain Fuji sand to hide the mesh. Then add enough potting mixture to cover the Fuji sand.

2 Remove the pine from its nursery pot and clean away soil from the surface and roots with tweezers.

3 Place the pine so that it bends to the left. Add soil and poke with a chopstick to fill air pockets with soil.

4 Use the plant mister to dampen the sand while flattening it with the spatula. Soak the soil so that the moss will establish quickly.

5 Cut old growth away from the back of the moss and pat it around the pine. Build up the moss into rich masses, forming small hills that undulate.

6 Pour white granite into the gaps to create the impression of a stream. Let the shape of it meander through the moss to present the appearance of flowing water.

7 Use the plant mister to dampen the arrangement while flattening the stones with the spatula. Press them down to tidy up the shape, and finish by watering.

KESHIKI 25

Stones
and moss on
a tiny hill

The feeling of the landscape extends beyond the petite scale of the container. The key here is in arranging stones of different sizes, ranging from small to large. After laying the moss around the stones, be sure to fill in gaps with gravel.

RUSTIC STYLE

Japanese mountain moss (yamagoke)

2¼ inches by 1⅝ inches by ¾ inches tall

1 Thread aluminum wire through a piece of mesh placed in the bottom of the planter and pull the ends of the wire through the drainage hole, securing by bending the ends across the bottom.

2 Add coarse-grain Fuji sand to hide the mesh.

3 Add potting mixture up to the rim.

4 Use the plant mister to dampen the soil while flattening it with the spatula. Soak the soil so that the moss will establish quickly.

5 Position three stones that range from large to small in a triangular formation, paying attention to the shape of each stone.

6 Remove the old growth from the back of the moss and place it between the stones. Press the pieces down firmly with your fingers to fill the space between the rocks.

7 Pour Kurama sand into the gaps to form a decorative topdressing and suggest the presence of a stream.

MOCHIKOMI: A TREE OR GRASS THAT HAS BEEN RAISED IN A CONTAINER FOR MORE THAN ONE YEAR.

KESHIKI 26

A leafy garden to restore your senses

Linger over this small garden filled with light. Place the ash seedling to the rear and then find the best place for the stone before covering the ground with moss. A decorative topdressing of Kurama sand finishes this graceful, elegant garden.

JAPANESE STYLE

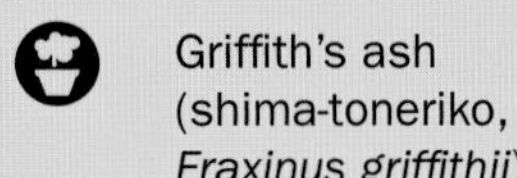

Griffith's ash (shima-toneriko, *Fraxinus griffithii*)

Japanese mountain moss (yamagoke)

3 inches in diameter by 1½ inches tall

1 Secure drainage mesh in the bottom of the container and add enough coarse-grain Fuji sand to hide the mesh. Then add enough potting mixture to hide the Fuji sand.

2 Remove the ash from its nursery pot and clean away soil from the surface and roots with tweezers. Be careful not to injure the roots.

3 Place the seedling in the left rear of the container and position it so that the branches extend to the right and the left. Add soil and poke with a chopstick to fill any air pockets with soil.

4 Use the plant mister to dampen the soil while flattening it with the spatula. Decide on where to place three stones. Once you've determined the locations, remove two of the stones and lay the moss in place.

5 With the moss spread on the soil, return the two stones to their positions.

6 Pour Kurama sand into the gaps as a decorative topdressing, turning the pot as you do this.

7 Use the plant mister to moisten the sand while flattening it with the spatula. Finish by watering.

MOTOFUKI: A BRANCH THAT SPROUTS (BREAKS THROUGH) FROM THE ROOT OF A TREE.

KESHIKI 27

The slender line of a tree in a white pot

Let moss cover the base of the tree as though holding it in its grip. Yasazuna stones suggest the presence of a stream, so evocative you can almost hear it.

MINIMALIST STYLE

Japanese zelkova (keyaki, *Zelkova serrata*)

velvet moss (birodogoke)

3¼ inches in diameter by 2 inches tall

1 Secure drainage mesh in the bottom of the container and add enough coarse-grain Fuji sand to hide the mesh. Then add enough potting mixture to hide the Fuji sand.

2 Remove the zelkova from its nursery pot and clean away soil from the surface and roots with tweezers.

3 Place the zelkova in the left rear of the container and add soil. Hold the seedling between your fingers so that the soil doesn't dislodge it.

4 Poke the soil with a chopstick to fill air pockets and form a solid mound of soil. Continue to support the seedling with your hand to keep it from slipping out of place.

5 Use the plant mister to dampen the soil while flattening it with the spatula.

6 Remove old growth from the back of the moss and spread it at the base of the zelkova. Use the chopstick to press the edges of the moss toward the center.

7 Pour yasazuna stones into the gaps to form a decorative topdressing. Use the plant mister to moisten the sand while pressing it down with the spatula. Finish by watering.

NE-BARI: DESCRIBES THE STATE OF ROOT DEVELOPMENT. ALSO, THE EXPOSURE OF THICK ROOTS ABOVE THE GROUND.

NE-TSURANARI: MULTIPLE TREES THAT ARE CONNECTED BY THE ROOTS.

KESHIKI 28

Reliving a climb to a lone tree on a mountaintop

JAPANESE STYLE

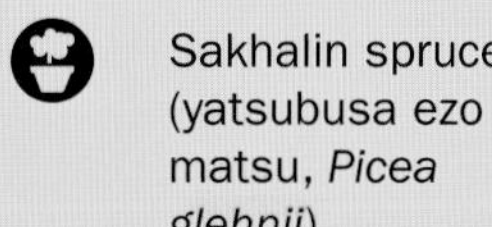

Sakhalin spruce (yatsubusa ezo matsu, *Picea glehnii*)

Japanese mountain moss (yamagoke)

5 inches by 2¾ inches by ¾ inch tall

1 Secure drainage mesh in the bottom of the container and then add coarse-grain Fuji sand to hide the mesh.

2 Add enough potting mixture to cover the Fuji sand. Since this is a flat container, the soil should be spread evenly over the entire area.

The stones in this bonsai recreate the feeling of rough-cut boulders. The light Kurama sand makes the scenery appear to float.

3 Remove the spruce seedling from its nursery pot. If the roots have spread and the plant is difficult to remove, plunge your tweezers into the soil at a few places around the pot to loosen the roots and free the seedling.

4 Use the tweezers to clean away soil from the plant's surface and roots. Untangle the roots carefully, without damaging them.

5 Once you have removed as much soil as you can, cut the roots so that they are slightly longer than the height of the tree.

SAIKEI: LITERALLY, "PLANTED SCENERY"—THE CREATION OF A LIVING LANDSCAPE PAINTING OR A NATURAL SCENE DEPICTED IN MINIATURE, BY DESIGNING WITH PLANTS AND STONES.

6 Place the spruce in the left rear and spread the roots over the entire container.

7 Fill the entire container with more soil to cover the roots and use a chopstick to poke the soil firmly and fill in air pockets.

8 Use the plant mister to dampen the soil and then flatten it with the spatula.

9 When the soil is uniformly moist, place the stones. Think of a mountain and position the stones as though they had rolled down a cliff to land in place. Remember the general rule about using an odd number of stones.

10 Spread moss around the tree. Create a grade like a mountain slope. Use the chopstick to press the edges of the moss toward the center of the container.

11 In the remaining gaps, add Kurama sand as a topdressing. Use the plant mister to moisten, smooth with the spatula, and finish by watering.

A stream meandering between mountain slopes

KESHIKI 29

RUSTIC STYLE

round-leaved cyclamen (*Cyclamen coum*)

Japanese mountain moss (yamagoke)

4 inches in diameter by 1¾ inches tall

1 Secure drainage mesh in the bottom of the container and add enough coarse-grain Fuji sand to hide the mesh. Next add enough potting soil to cover the Fuji sand.

2 Remove the cyclamen from its nursery pot and clean off soil with the tweezers. Place the plant in the left rear of the container so that the tuber is seated above the soil.

This bonsai invites a refreshing breeze into your room. Plant the cyclamen so that the tuber on top of the root peeks out above the soil. Create hills of grass and stone with Kurama sand running between the elements like a flow of fresh spring water.

3 Add soil and poke with a chopstick to compact the soil and fill in air pockets.

4 Use the plant mister to dampen the soil and then flatten it with the spatula.

5 Position seven stones to achieve a good balance. Imagine you are forming grassy hills and craggy mountains as you place the stones.

6 Remove the old growth from the back of the moss and build up a gentle knoll around the planting. Placing a stone on top of the mound of moss will bring extra potency to the landscape.

7 Add Kurama sand to places where bare soil is still exposed to create the sense of a stream flowing through the scene. Smooth the sand while spraying with the plant mister and then water to finish.

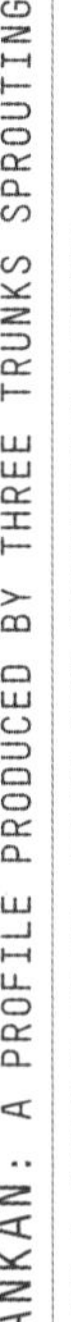

DIFFERENT MATERIALS FOR CONTRAST AND EMBELLISHMENT

Besides stones and sand, you can also try working with charcoal or soil to lend a different mood or quality to the topdressing on your bonsai. Experiment with textures and colors to complement a room's décor or for a change from the expected.

1. Charcoal. Besides the visual interest of the black grains, charcoal also has a cleansing effect on the room, acting as an air purifier. Perfect for living or dining rooms.

2. Kiryu soil. This is an acidic soil that has the advantage of discouraging weeds. Other plants won't grow in it, so you can enjoy the same landscape for a long time.

3. Kanuma soil. This soil has very good water-retention properties. Generally, topdressings are used in bonsai to hide the soil, and Kanuma serves that purpose as well. When dry, it appears whitish, but it deepens in color when watered.

This bonsai uses Kanuma soil as the topdressing. When watered, the deepened color weaves together the moss and the soil's exquisite texture.

KESHIKI 30

Tall trees
and rough stones in
a deep forest

MINIMALIST STYLE

 Japanese cypress (hinoki, *Chamaecyparis obtusa*)

 Japanese mountain moss (yamagoke)

 4 inches in diameter by 1½ inches tall

1 Secure drainage mesh in the bottom of the container and add enough coarse-grain Fuji sand to hide the mesh. Next, add enough potting mixture to cover the Fuji sand.

2 Remove three cypress trees from their nursery pots and clean away soil from the surface and roots with tweezers.

Applying the principle of linear perspective lends a sense of depth to this bonsai; trees take on the proportions of a forest. Lava on the ground adds grit and brawn and brings a rugged outdoorsy look to the arrangement.

3 Determine the relative sizes of the trees: small, medium, large. Place the large- and medium-sized trees closer to the front, and the smaller one farther away in a formation that produces a triangle with unequal sides.

4 Poke the soil with a chopstick to fill in air pockets. Hold the trees in place with your fingers to keep them from becoming displaced.

5 Use the plant mister to dampen the soil while smoothing it with the spatula. Keep spraying until the water has soaked the soil.

6 Pinch off old growth from the back of the moss and cut a slit to make it easier to lay the moss around the base of the trees. Use the chopstick to push the moss into shape.

7 In the spaces between the plants, add coarse-grain Fuji sand as well as pieces of lava for a scraggy texture. Spray with water while smoothing the surface with the spatula to finish.

SASHIKI: THE CUTTING OF A BRANCH TIP AND PLACING IT IN SOIL SO THAT IT ROOTS.

A moonlit scene at water's edge in a whimsical container

KESHIKI 31

EURO STYLE

- Japanese black pine (kuromatsu, *Pinus thunbergii*),
- Japanese mountain moss (yamagoke)

- 2¾ inches in diameter by 2½ inches tall

1 Secure drainage mesh in the bottom of the container and add coarse-grain Fuji sand to cover the mesh. Next, add enough potting mixture to cover the Fuji sand.

2 Remove the pine seedling from its nursery pot and clean away soil from the surface and roots with tweezers.

3 Position the pine in the container and add soil. Poke the soil with a chopstick to fill in air pockets and secure the plant.

Nachiguro stones convey the tones of a rocky shoreline, glistening darkly when wet with water. Notice how the spiky upward flare of the pine needles emphasizes the other shapes in the arrangement, offsetting the rounded forms with bristling tension.

SENTEI: PRUNING, THE REMOVAL OF BRANCHES THAT ARE SPINDLY, TOO VIGOROUS, OR OVERLY ABUNDANT IN ORDER TO MAINTAIN AND IMPROVE THE SHAPE OF A TREE.

4 Use the plant mister to dampen the soil while smoothing it with the spatula. Pinch off old growth from the back of the moss and lay it around the base of the tree.

5 Use the chopstick to push the moss away from the edge and toward the center. Hold the tree to keep it from moving and press the moss securely into the soil.

6 Where there is bare soil, spread Nachiguro stones as a topdressing.

7 Spray with water while pressing the stones into the soil to set them in place. Wetting these stones creates a sense of calm, like being in a quiet tea garden.

A SELECTION OF TEXTILES THAT ENHANCE KESHIKI BONSAI

The colors of bonsai tend to be subdued. This is where textiles can play an important role. In mini bonsai, since we are dealing with pots that are quite small, the textile needn't be much larger than a coaster, just enough to add a bit of color, either contrasting or complementing the tones in the bonsai. Pictured here are some of my favorites, which you can see are sometimes in the form of small cushions or heavy weaves that add an element of texture. Experiment with patterns and palettes that set off the bonsai in your interior space and express your own personal style.

SHAKAN: A TREE CONFIGURED SO THAT THE TRUNK SLANTS IN ONE DIRECTION.

SUTE ISHI: STONES RANDOMLY SCATTERED ON THE ROAD BY RIVERS IN THE MOUNTAINS.

Ritsuko Sato

TEXTILE DYER

Ritsuko Sato, proprietor of Atelier Couleur (www.ateliercouleur.com), is active in a number of fields from kimonos to accessories to linens and homewares, and since 2001 has been producing clothing from raw silk. After graduating from the Tokyo Senshoku Art College, she completed a further course of studies at Vantan Textile Design School, studying with textile artist Keiko Otsuki. She has energetically participated in solo shows and group exhibitions throughout Japan.

The first time I met Sato was in 2003 at a department store exhibition in western Japan. On first impression this tall, slender woman dazzles you with eyes of arresting sparkle. Added to this, it made my heart pound to think that this was the person responsible for the color-saturated textiles produced one after another in a stream of creative productivity.

The colors that Sato achieves are neither too pop nor too somber; for all their depth, there is something understated and restrained about them. Her colors are graceful—even when they are vibrant they maintain an unobtrusiveness that invites you in. Looking at the finished items made up of those textiles, you realize that they have the remarkable quality of being able to melt into any sort of interior décor. I was immediately struck by how well these would work with keshiki bonsai, bolstering the plantings with added presence and impact.

Sato's atelier is in a narrow four-story building situated in a quiet residential area. The first floor serves as both her showroom and shop, the second floor is her living space, the third floor is her dyeing workroom, and the fourth floor functions as both office and design studio. The showroom displays clothing, cushions, bags, and other items. Light from the window plays on the colors of the textiles so that they seem to glow and even radiate. In my shop, I display keshiki bonsai on small pieces of cloth; to add vibrancy to the limited colors of bonsai, Sato's textiles are exactly perfect.

The day I went to interview her, Sato, without the slightest ado, prepared a delightful meal of rice cooked in an earthen pot, served with a dish simmered in a delicate broth. The meal offered by this magician of color was both simple and redolent of home, like a whiff of mother's cooking. For me, the colors of her textiles will forever remind me of her kind hospitality—after all, it's the feelings we attach to beautiful things that make them even more meaningful.

Sato's work, on display in her showroom on the first floor. Handmade goods together with an assortment of colorful textiles are shown in a beautifully composed display.

Brushes neatly lined up in the work area, all different types for different processes, all looking well-used and cared for.

Keshiki bonsai composed of camellia and moss, placed before a silk organdy hanging dyed by Sato. The richness of the textile sets off the form and color of the plants.

Sato checking the colors of textiles she has just finished dyeing. This is also where she designs her clothing, bags, and other handmade articles.

Sato treating me to her home-cooked meal, modestly remarking, "This is all I could come up with."

Scarves combining two brilliant shades of color.

BONSAI IN NOVEL CONTAI

If you've ever thought that you cannot buy any more expensive containers, or you want a more fun, offbeat, unexpected look for your bonsai, put your creativity to use in finding all sorts of novel containers around your home. As long as there is a drainage hole in the bottom, anything goes. Try something different to bring a whole new dimension to the enjoyment of mini bonsai.

NERS

KESHIKI 32

A reimagined coffee cup

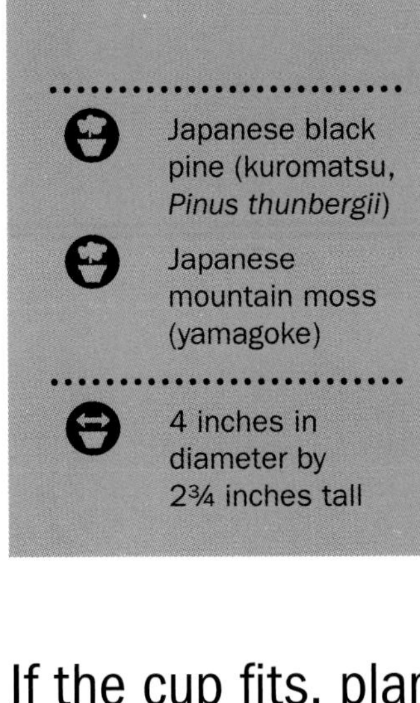

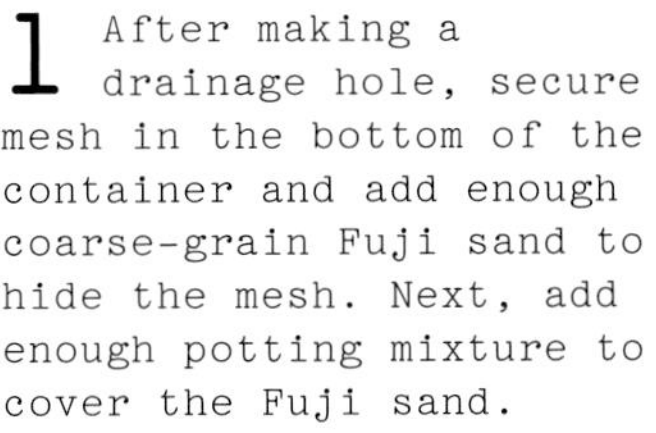

1 After making a drainage hole, secure mesh in the bottom of the container and add enough coarse-grain Fuji sand to hide the mesh. Next, add enough potting mixture to cover the Fuji sand.

2 Remove the pine from its nursery pot and clean away soil from the surface and roots with tweezers.

If the cup fits, plant it! This is a great way to recycle interesting tableware, bringing new life to old favorites in your collection. All you need to do is drill a hole in the base of the cup. The scale is just right for nurturing a small piece of nature.

3 Place the tree in the cup, positioning it so as to best show off the shape of the branch. Add soil. For the best effect, plant the tree with its needles facing upward.

4 Poke the soil with a chopstick to fill in air pockets with soil. Hold the tree in place by supporting the base of it with your fingers.

5 Use the plant mister to dampen the soil while smoothing it with the spatula.

TACHI-EDA: A BRANCH THAT EMERGES PARALLEL TO THE TRUNK AND GROWS UPWARD FROM THE MAIN BRANCH.

6 Pinch off old growth from the back of the moss and cut a slit to make it easier to lay the moss around the base of the pine. Form a raised mound, conveying the sense of a hill.

7 Use the chopstick to push overhanging bits of moss toward the center of the cup.

8 As a topdressing, add fine-grain Fuji sand to areas of bare soil. Spray with water while smoothing the surface with the spatula, and then water to finish.

ADDING A DRAINAGE HOLE

The biggest problem with using a household container as a planter is the lack of a drainage hole. If the container is tin, it is easy enough to make a hole using a nail and a hammer. But for ceramics or glass, it is useful to have an electric hand drill with a set of diamond drill bits to easily drill the hole without fear of breakage. With this one purchase, you can vastly widen your choice of planters.

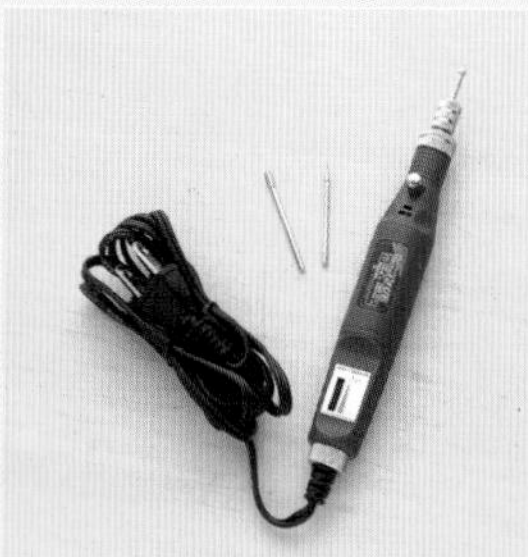

You can buy a mini electric drill set at home improvement stores or on the Web. Look for one that lets you change the bit according to the material you're drilling. The pencil-type design is especially easy to grip.

1 Drilling produces abrasion heat, so first apply water to the area where you want to make a hole.

2 Insert the smallest diamond drill bit you have into the hand drill and turn it on.

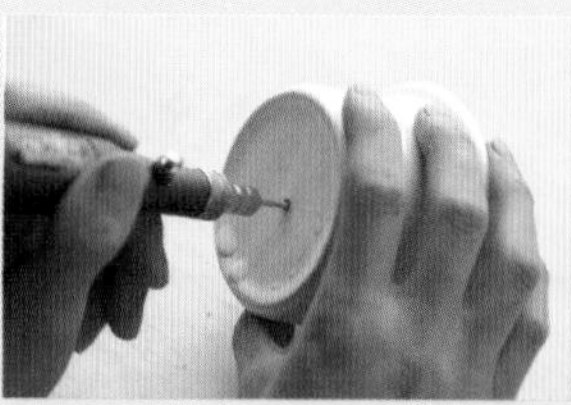

3 Once you've drilled through, use a larger bit to grind the hole to the right size.

KESHIKI 33

A repurposed jelly mold

- variegated Mt. Fuji rockcress (fu-iri hatazao, *Arabis serrata* 'Variegata')
- Japanese mountain moss (yamagoke)

- 2½ inches in diameter by 1½ inches tall

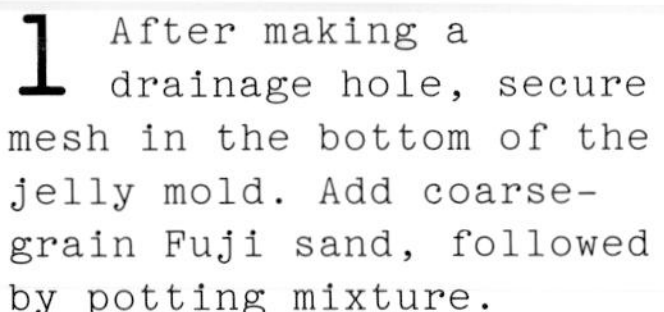

1 After making a drainage hole, secure mesh in the bottom of the jelly mold. Add coarse-grain Fuji sand, followed by potting mixture.

2 Remove the rockcress from its nursery pot by pressing the bottom of the pot and supporting the plant in the palm of your hand as it is released.

Worn-out jelly molds that no longer serve a purpose in the kitchen look beautiful when paired with variegated plants. All you need is one drainage hole. In addition to the charming form of the molds, the gleaming surface supplies a bright counterbalance to the subdued tones of plants. These two molds will dress up a dining table as a radiant centerpiece.

3 Remove all the outer soil with your fingers.

4 Place the rockcress in the form and slowly fill the container with soil, starting from the sides. Hold the seedling in place with your fingers to keep it from moving.

5 Use a chopstick to poke the soil, tamping it down to remove air pockets. Next, spray water while smoothing the soil with the spatula.

6 Remove old growth from the back of the moss and place it bit by bit around the base of the plant.

7 Use the chopstick to push overhanging bits of moss toward the center of the form to create a gentle hill. Finish by covering any bare soil with fine-grain Fuji sand.

8 In another jelly mold, prepared with a hole and drainage mesh, add soil to the brim and spread moss over the top. Fill gaps with fine-grain Fuji sand as a decorative topdressing.

KESHIKI 34

A new life for a ramekin

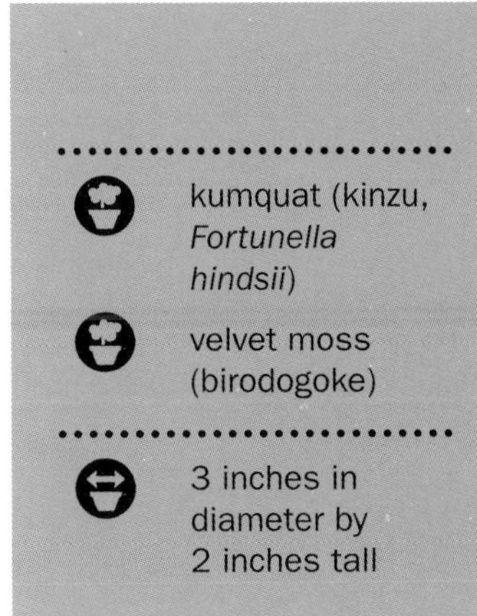

1 After making a drainage hole, secure mesh in the bottom of the container. Add coarse-grain Fuji sand, followed by potting mixture.

2 Remove the kumquat from its nursery pot by pressing the bottom of the pot to help release it.

The brilliant green of velvet moss against the clean white pleated surface of a ramekin makes for a dynamic study in contrasts. Add to this the warm tones of kumquat that ripens in the winter for a bracing mix of sensations floating through the air.

3 Remove soil clinging to the surface of the seedling and its roots with tweezers. Gently untangle the roots, taking care not to damage them.

4 Place the kumquat in the center of the dish and add soil. Support the base of the plant with your hand so that it doesn't become dislodged.

TORIKI: PLANT PROPAGATION BY LAYERING, WHICH PRODUCES A NEW TREE FROM AN EXISTING TRUNK OR BRANCH THAT IS BENT SO THAT IT COMES IN CONTACT WITH THE SOIL.

5 Use a chopstick to poke the soil, tamping it down to remove air pockets. Here also, hold the plant with your hand so that it doesn't get jostled out of place as you firmly compress the soil.

6 Mist the soil as you smooth it with the spatula. Make sure that water penetrates the soil thoroughly to provide a good base for the moss to establish.

7 Remove old growth from the back of the moss with scissors and place it around the base of the kumquat. Try piecing together small portions of the moss to produce a more complex ground cover.

8 Press excess moss away from the edge of the dish with the chopstick and finish with a good watering.

KESHIKI 35

The possibilities
of an empty box

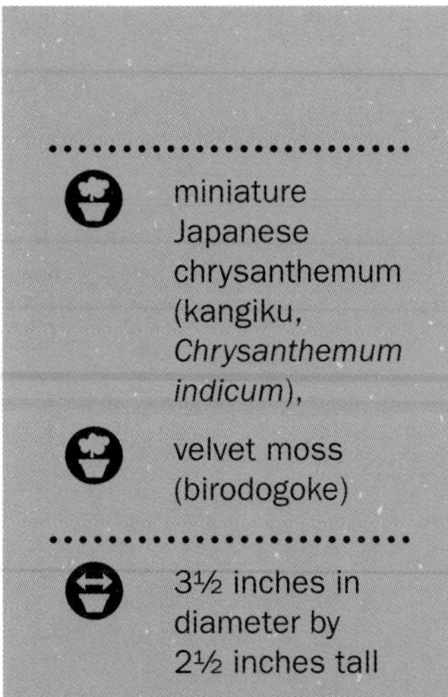

1 After making a drainage hole, secure mesh in the bottom of the container. Add coarse-grain Fuji sand followed by potting mixture until the box is a third full.

2 Take the chrysanthemum out of its nursery pot and remove soil from the surface and roots with your fingers.

A stylish bonsai lives in the leftover packaging from a wheel of cheese. For miniature Japanese chrysanthemums, secure the roots firmly and position the plant so that the part aboveground forms a forest of flowers. Be sure to support the stems with your fingers when laying the moss on the ground.

3 Position the plant in the box and then add soil. This will be easier to accomplish if you hold the seedling with your hand so that it doesn't move.

4 Use a chopstick to poke the soil, tamping it down to remove air pockets. Hold the plant at the base so that you don't interfere with the position as you work.

5 Mist the soil with water as you smooth it with the spatula.

6 Remove old growth from the back of the moss with scissors and lay the moss around the base of the chrysanthemum. Use the chopstick to push the moss away from the edges.

7 Add fine-grain Fuji sand as a topdressing over areas with bare soil, turning the box as you work.

8 Spray with water once again, smoothing the sand with the spatula, and finish by watering.

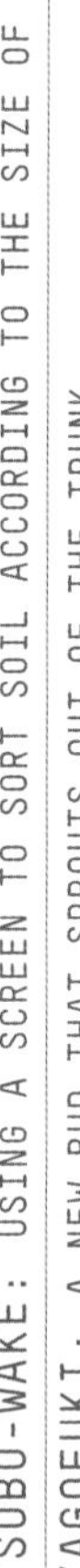

KESHIKI 36

An empty can transformed

- multiflora rose (noibara, *Rosa multiflora*)
- Japanese mountain moss (yamagoke)

- 2¾ inches in diameter by 2¾ inches tall

1 After making a drainage hole, secure mesh in the bottom of the container. Add coarse-grain Fuji sand followed by potting mixture until the can is a third full.

2 Remove the rose from its nursery pot by squeezing the pot on the bottom to release the seedling.

Container repurposing opens up new vistas for plant enthusiasts. There is great visual resonance between the can and the multiflora rose, whether it's in bloom or bearing fruit. It's easy to make a drainage hole using just a nail and a hammer.

3 Clean off soil from the surface and roots with tweezers. Work carefully so as not to damage the roots.

4 Place the cleaned rose roots in the can and position the plant to optimum advantage. Support the plant in your hand as you then add soil.

5 Use a chopstick to poke the soil, tamping it down to remove air pockets. Hold the base of the plant with your hand as you work until the soil secures it in place.

6 Mist the soil as you smooth it with the spatula. Make sure that water penetrates the soil thoroughly to provide a good base for the moss to establish.

7 Remove old growth from the back of the moss and place it so it surrounds the base of the rose. Create visual interest by piecing together small clumps of moss to produce a hilly terrain. Press excess moss away from the edge of the can with the chopstick and finish with a good watering.

KESHIKI 37

A new use for a plastic tray

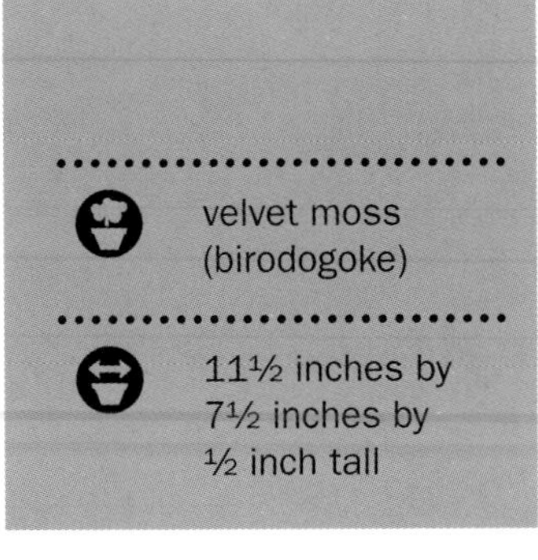

1 Punch four drainage holes with a hammer and a nail. It's best if the holes are in different places on the bottom so that water can drain easily. Then add potting mixture.

2 Mist with water and smooth the soil, patting it down with the spatula so that it is the same height over the entire area.

A rectangular plastic tray holds a scene reminiscent of tiny islands in the sea as they appear out the window of an airplane. Position mounds of moss to simulate the topography of islands. Fill in the spaces with Fuji sand to suggest a tranquil sea.

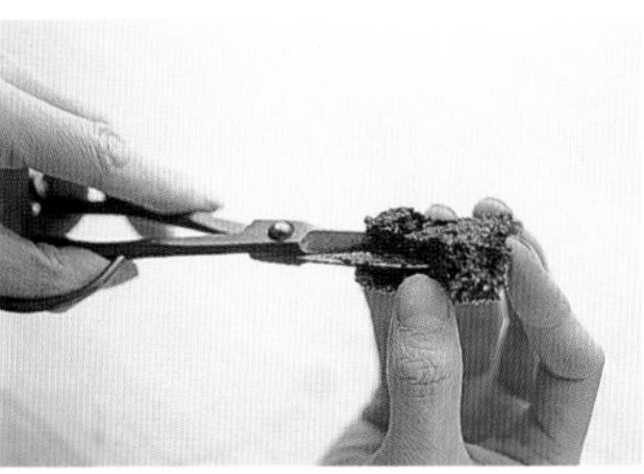

3 Cut off old growth from the back of the moss with scissors.

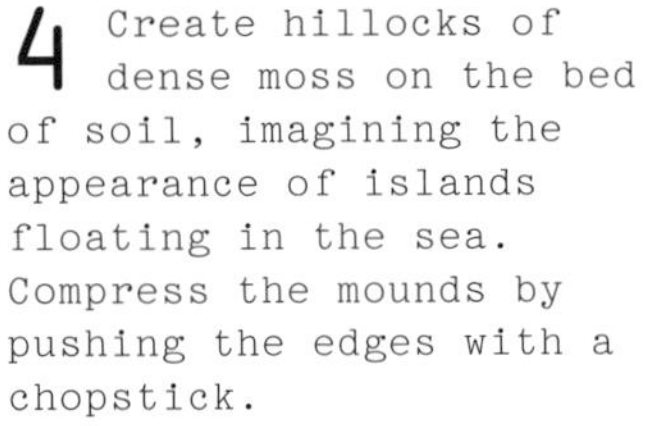

4 Create hillocks of dense moss on the bed of soil, imagining the appearance of islands floating in the sea. Compress the mounds by pushing the edges with a chopstick.

5 Once you have finished laying the moss in place, cover the bare soil with a topdressing of fine-grain Fuji sand that has been run through a sieve.

6 Mist with water as you smooth the ground with the spatula. Work patiently across the wide area, firming the sand to complete the project.

EXPLORING THE POSSIBILITIES FOR KESHIKI BONSAI CONTAINERS

I would like to introduce you to some different types of containers, sold specifically for bonsai, including some that have been used in this book. You can find containers made from all types of materials—ceramic, metal, glass. Artists make many of these, so their prices are higher, but they have a presence that gives them character. Any of them would bring the element of artistic design to your bonsai arrangements, either balancing or contrasting with the plant materials you have chosen. (The containers in these photographs are all available for sale at my store, Sinajina.)

Ceramic containers. These impart a sense of stillness while at the same time exuding warmth. The rounded shapes embrace the plants with a quiet unobtrusiveness. A small seedling planted in a small pot feels much bigger, since it fills its space so robustly.

Metal containers. The gold-colored containers are actually made of brass, and the silver from tin. While they might appear cold at first glance, they convey an exquisite sharpness when paired with bonsai, combining in a way that speaks to a modern sensibility. Gorgeous without being garish.

Glass containers. Glass containers are quite new for use as bonsai pots, adding an unusual, unexpected texture to nature sculpture such as bonsai. Since the soil shows through, a colored glass may be the better choice. Perfect for eclectic interiors that fuse elements from East and West, glass vessels blend into the mix with ease.

Akiko Tsuruta

GLASS ARTIST

Akiko Tsuruta was born in Nagoya and studied at the Tokyo Glass Art Institute after graduating from Musashino Art University Junior College of Art and Design. She has won numerous prizes at Tokyo glass art exhibitions and Japanese craft shows, and participates annually in solo and group shows. Tsuruta might at first seem like the essence of a proper Japanese woman—calm, poised, and intellectual. Still, it is my impression that she is in fact a passionate person with great inner strength at her core.

I met Tsuruta through Hisao Iwashimizu at an artist's show. Even though it was the first time we'd met, when we started talking over drinks and shared ideas about art, it became clear that we were completely of one mind. The fusion of glass and bonsai was something no one had tried thus far–in Japan, the idea of having the soil visible through the container is unappealing–but meeting with Tsuruta was like throwing open a new door. In her mind, the color of the glass would hide the soil while the light-infused material would add a luminosity to the finished arrangement.

She got to work on a piece right away, and it was amazing how well it went with bonsai. Thus was born a highly individualistic style of bonsai, exclusive to Sinajina and overflowing with originality. Glass, which the Japanese associate with summer for its welcome icy look, becomes an all-season material when used as a container for bonsai.

Tsuruta studied design in the beginning, but as her interest in glass grew, she moved on to a school specializing in glass. What inspires her is a love for pieces that are heavy and stout, pieces that contrast the fragility of the material with solidity of form. Her home has the feeling of a gallery with antique furnishings placed in spare surroundings. Crystalline glass artworks decorate the shelves and tops of chests, creating fantasy worlds of sea and night sky in their glimmering depths.

"For glass, transparency is life. The pieces retain their beauty as long as they are polished and taken care of." Tsuruta's ideas about glass and the art she makes will continue to fuse with keshiki bonsai–and who knows? It's exciting to think of the new doors that may yet open.

Raised dots on the exterior of these cups provide tactile interest when held in one's hands.

A vessel whose original coloring earned it an award at a craft exhibition holds a bonsai of horsetails and multiflora roses. The deep color, as mysterious and brilliant as the Milky Way, hides the soil and gives the bonsai a clean, sparkling finish that looks beautiful as room decoration.

Work by Akiko Tsuruta: An objet d'art functions as a perfume bottle.

This bowl was conceived around the image of the ocean floor.

Talking about glass, we shift our conversation to her dieting strategies and erupt in roars of laughter.

PLANTS FOR KESHIKI BONSAI

EVERGREEN TREES

Chinese juniper (shinpaku, *Juniperus chinesis*)

Cypress family. Peeling away the bark on the trunk and branches reveals white wood in a styling technique called jin. Chinese juniper also lends itself to the technique of shari in which a part of the trunk is allowed to wither and decay. Both methods yield deadwood, giving the sense of a very old tree.

CARE: If the jin or shari becomes soiled, use a toothbrush to wash the area with water. The plant can be placed outdoors from spring to late autumn, and in winter brought back inside or placed under the eaves.

Dwarf Japanese cedar (himesugi, *Cryptomeria japonica*)

Cedar family. Cedar is a fast-growing tree, extending straight upward. This is a miniature variety. The trunk is lushly covered with needle-shaped leaves.

CARE: Grow in a place with ample sunlight and good ventilation. Water well when the surface of the soil is dry.

Griffith's ash (shima-toneriko, *Fraxinus griffithii*)

Olive family. Dense foliage and small leaves make this tree a bonsai favorite. It is evergreen to semi-deciduous, depending on winter cold. Ash is the wood used for baseball bats and has a cleansing effect on the air, making it ideal for growing indoors.

CARE: Grow where there is ample sunlight. The plant likes moist soil and does poorly in an extremely dry environment. Be sure to water well during the summertime.

The plants introduced here are easily available and intended for the beginner. For the most part, they are plants that have been used in this book. I have divided them into trees, shrubs, and herbaceous perennials, and further categorized the trees and shrubs as evergreen or deciduous.

Japanese black pine (kuromatsu, *Pinus thunbergii*)

Pine family. Named for its dark-colored trunk, this tree symbolizes masculinity because of its hardy endurance through every kind of weather. Its trunk develops thick tortoiseshell-shaped scales that eventually peel and fall off.

CARE: Water often; if the surface of the soil has dried out, be sure to water generously. The roots remain alive even if the needles brown, so be sure to continue to provide ample water.

Japanese cypress (hinoki, *Chamaecyparis obtusa*)

Cypress family. Rubbing cypress sticks together was once used for creating sparks and led to an old name for cypress, "the fire tree." Cypress grows by creeping along the tops of rocky crags where the wind hits it.

CARE: Cypress grows quickly and needs pruning to control its shape. Treat to prevent damage from pests or disease.

Japanese red pine (akamatsu, *Pinus densiflora*)

Pine family. As the name suggests, the trunk of this tree is a reddish brown. With age, the bark develops fissures, giving an effect reminiscent of tortoiseshell. The foliage is needle-shaped, and the seed-bearing structure is the familiar pinecone. This tree symbolizes femininity.

CARE: Grow in a place with ample sunlight and good drainage. When styling the branches, prune so that light hits the main trunk.

EVERGREEN TREES CONTINUED

Japanese white pine (goyomatsu, ***Pinus parviflora***)

Pine family. Its nickname "five-needle pine" is derived from the fact that its needles, each about 1¼ inches to 2½ inches long, are bundled in groups of five. This gives the impression of volume and is popular as a portent of good luck.

CARE: This tree is generally resilient to drying out but grows slowly. Be mindful that dieback can occur if branches touch each other.

Kumquat (kinzu, *Fortunella hindsii*)

Citrus family. Being a dwarf variety with thick-growing leaves and branches, this plant lends itself well to bonsai. In late summer or early autumn, after flowers stop blossoming, yellow- or orange-colored fruit forms.

CARE: The plant is sensitive to cold, so keep it indoors if the temperature dips below 59F (15C). Return outdoors in late spring when there is no more threat of frost.

Sakhalin spruce (yatsubusa ezo matsu, ***Picea glehnii***)

Pine family. This spruce is seen along the ski slopes on Japan's northern island from which it takes its name. Very resilient to cold, with lovely yellow buds appearing on the branches in late spring.

CARE: Grow in a place with ample sunlight and good ventilation. Does not do well with extensive pruning; instead, style by removing branches that are overcrowded.

DECIDUOUS TREES

Asian red oak (konara, *Quercus serrata*)

Beech family. The familiar acorn-bearing tree rarely bears fruit when used in bonsai, where it is appreciated for its deep green foliage that turns color in the fall. When the branches are pruned, the plant gives a pleasant sense of coolness that is a welcome sight in summer heat.

CARE: Replant in early spring. It is important to remove the plant from its pot since if left alone, the root will grow too thick.

Chinese elm (nire-keyaki, *Ulmus parvifolia*)

Elm family. This tree is admired for its charming buds that sprout in autumn and its yellow autumn coloring.

CARE: Grows well in sun and shade; easy to take care of. Prune growth, leaving two or three nodes to encourage small branches to increase.

Japanese hornbeam (soro, *Carpinus japonica*)

Birch family. This tree is a very common sight in woodlands and parks; there is sure to be one in your vicinity.

CARE: Hardy and easy to grow, hornbeam needs only to be protected from summer sunlight. Place under the eaves or in another shaded spot to avoid burning the leaves.

DECIDUOUS TREES CONTINUED

Japanese maple (momiji, *Acer palmatum*)

Maple family. Perfect for bonsai intended to resemble a woodland, wild and natural. The maple provides year-round visual interest, starting with a burst of new buds in spring, brilliant autumn foliage, and the bare bones of the tree's structure in winter.

CARE: The time to replant is when the red buds appear. For mini bonsai, repot once every one or two years.

Japanese persimmon (kaki/fudegaki, *Diospyros kaki*)

Ebony family. The leaves turn a lovely color in the autumn, and once they have fallen, the color of the fruit begins to deepen. Flowers are pale yellow, bell-shaped, and about ½ inch wide, with four petals that bend backward.

CARE: Take indoors during the winter to protect the plant from wind. Cold, dry wind can cause dieback and reduce the amount of fruit produced the following year.

Japanese zelkova (keyaki, *Zelkova serrata*)

Elm family. This broad-leaved tree is representative of Japan. Leaves turn yellow in the fall. In bonsai, the plant lends itself to elegant arrangements.

CARE: Guard against powdery mildew on young seedlings. The shape of the tree will develop as the tree grows, so avoid excessive pruning.

EVERGREEN SHRUBS

Wax tree (haze, *Rhus succedanea*)

Sumac family. This tree is popular for its impressive autumn coloring. Many trees can be massed together because the plant does not branch much. People with sensitive skin may develop a rash from contact with this plant and should therefore determine if they are allergic before choosing to grow it.

CARE: Hardy and resilient to leaf-burn; easy to grow.

African bush daisy (ma-gareto kosumosu, *Euryops* species)

Daisy family. This low-growing evergreen bush is resilient to cold with dramatically notched leaves. Yellow flowers bloom from midsummer through late autumn.

CARE: Suffers in extreme heat and dryness; place under eaves or an otherwise cool location in the summertime. Watch out for spider mites and cockroaches.

Camellia (tsubaki, *Camellia japonica*)

Camellia family. These plants, which can be grown outdoors as large shrubs or small trees, are known for their glossy leaves and brightly colored flowers. The word in Japanese is said to derive from the fact that it has thick leaves (atsubaki).

CARE: Camellia is hardy and relatively resilient to cold, although prolonged subfreezing temperatures will kill it. It does poorly in excessive humidity; be careful not to overwater. When pruning, cut at the branch joint.

EVERGREEN SHRUBS CONTINUED

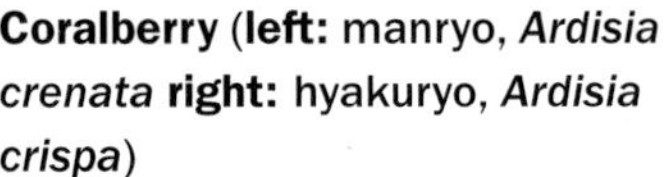

Coralberry (**left:** manryo, *Ardisia crenata* **right:** hyakuryo, *Ardisia crispa*)

Myrsine family. The genus *Ardisia* includes about 250 species of shrubs and small trees, but the two species known commonly as coralberry are favorites for bonsai. Both feature blooms of delicate white flowers and berries that redden in late autumn and last until mid-spring of the following year.

CARE: The plant is sensitive to dry environments with cold wind and strong sunlight, so pay attention to placement and watering. Grow in partial shade. Prune branches that grow too long, though this sometimes inhibits flowering for two to three years.

Heavenly bamboo (nanten, *Nandina domestica*)

Barberry family. Heavenly bamboo is evergreen to semi-deciduous, depending on winter cold. As it gets colder, the red foliage color intensifies for a brilliant effect. Large clusters of creamy or pinkish white blossoms appear in late spring, followed by showy red berries.

CARE: The flowers do poorly in rain, so be sure to take this plant indoors or place under a shelter during wet spells. In early summer, cut overly long branches to the base.

Japanese andromeda (asebi, *Pieris japonica*)

Heath family. When written with Chinese characters, the name of this shrub is literally "drunken horse tree." It contains asebo toxin, which when ingested by a horse has a numbing effect on its nerves that causes a drunken-like state.

CARE: Grow in a place with filtered sunlight and be careful that the soil does not dry out. Cut off blossoms after flowering is over.

Japanese ardisia (yabukoji, *Ardisia japonica*)

Myrsine family. Like the coralberries, this plant produces small white flowers in summer and red berries from autumn through winter.

CARE: In midspring, prune branches that have grown too long. Keep in the shade during the summer, but place where it will get sunshine in winter.

Senryo (senryo, *Sarcandra glabra*)

Chloranthus family. Clusters of red berries appear from late autumn through winter, making it a favorite for the winter holidays, when its colors and abundance of fruit are considered lucky charms.

CARE: The plant dislikes cold and direct sunlight, so raise it in filtered or dappled shade. Be careful to keep it out of strong sunshine, which will burn the leaves.

Variegated Japanese andromeda (fu-iri asebi, *Pieris japonica* 'Variegata')

Heath family. This andromeda has spotted, patterned leaves that add interest to the plant.

CARE: Hardy and easy to grow, though it is best to avoid placing the plant where it is exposed to the strong rays of direct summer sunlight.

DECIDUOUS SHRUBS

Japanese beautyberry **(murasaki shikibu, *Callicarpa japonica*)**

Verbena family. The charm of this plant is in the bright purple berries that appear in great numbers on the branches in autumn. There is also a white variety, and recently a miniature with even smaller berries has appeared on the market.

CARE: Be sure to keep watering even after flowers bloom and until the berries form. Fertilize in spring and fall.

Multiflora rose (noibara, ***Rosa multiflora***)

Rose family. Pink or white flowers blossom in early summer, exuding a delightful fragrance, while red rosehips mature in autumn and last throughout the winter.

CARE: Grows well from bud cuttings. Recommended for beginners, since the plant can be multiplied by sowing the rosehips that form in winter before spring begins.

Variegated multiflora rose **(fu-iri noibara, *Rosa multiflora* 'Variegata')**

Rose family. White- to cream-colored patterning on the leaves adds extra decorative impact, particularly when the new buds open into pink blossoms.

CARE: As with the multiflora rose, this plant does well when grown from bud cuttings. Grow where there is good light and water drainage.

HERBACEOUS PERENNIALS

Azure bluet (hinaso, ***Houstonia caerulea***)

Madder family. At the tip of a slender stem, tiny flowers about ½ inch in diameter appear. The plant looks fragile but in fact is quite hardy, and the blooming season is long. Propagates well from its rhizome.

CARE: Feeding with a liquid fertilizer during the blooming season ensures continuous, healthy blossoms. Divide the roots when the plant grows large.

Bog rosemary (hime shakunage, ***Andromeda polifolia***)

Heath family. This perennial originally flourished in high mountain wetlands. During the summer, small jar-shaped, pinkish flowers appear at the tip of the stem, facing downward.

CARE: Raise in a place that remains cool in summer with good ventilation. Be conservative with fertilizer. Provide a windbreak in winter. Propagate by taking cuttings.

Coltsfoot (fukitanpopo, ***Tussilago farfara***)

Daisy family. Bright yellow flowers resembling dandelions appear on bare stems in early spring. The leaves in cross section resemble a colt's foot. In Japan the plant is popular as a bonsai for New Year's, believed to augur good luck, but it can be invasive or weedy and is banned in some parts of the United States.

CARE: Flowers will not open unless the plant is placed in sunlight. Once blooming is over, replant in a container slighter larger than the one it had been in.

HERBACEOUS PERENNIALS CONTINUED

Cremanthodium (hime-tsuwabuki, ***Cremanthodium campanulatum***)

Daisy family. Leaves of this evergreen perennial are thick and lustrous. It produces yellow flowers in late autumn.

CARE: Grow where there is good ventilation and partial shade.

Dwarf sweet flag (hime sekisho, ***Acorus gramineus***)

Sweet flag family. This plant grows wild along the banks of mountain streams. The rhizome is hard and has nodes as well as fragrance. Many small, spearhead-shaped, pale yellow blooms appear in spring.

CARE: Replant every two to three years and separate the roots. The shape can be improved by a single leaf-clipping session in late spring.

Golden leather fern **(ogonshida, *Acrostichum aureum*)**

Bracken family. While there are no blossoms on this plant, the foliage is lush and rich. For bonsai, these work well when used for the lacy carpet of green they produce.

CARE: Avoid direct sunlight and grow in soil with good drainage. Hardy and easy to grow; ideal for beginners. Be sparing with fertilizer.

Goldenthread (baika oren, *Coptis quinquefolia*)

Buttercup family. In early spring, purple-tinged flower stems appear, extending straight up from between the leaves. At the tip, a white flower very much like a plum blossom appears.

CARE: Grow where there is good ventilation in the summer. Adding fertilizer in spring and autumn will assure a good annual display of blooms.

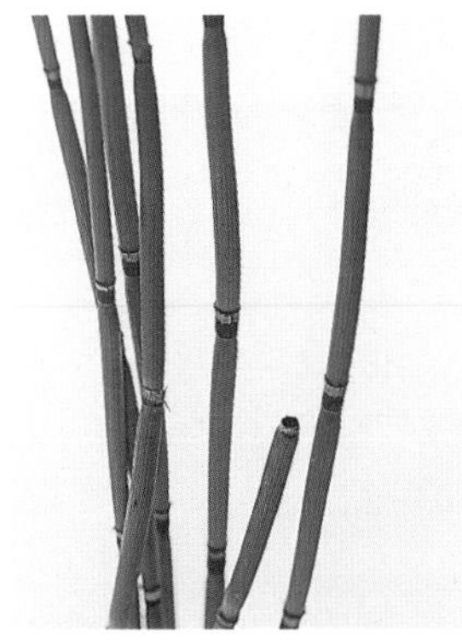

Horsetail (tokusa, *Equisetum hyemale*)

Horsetail family. This ornamental perennial can be planted for its sheer visual pleasure. In the wild, this reed grows in cold mountainous climates. The stem is hollow and there is a black pattern on the nodes.

CARE: Cut back to the ground in early spring to encourage new sprouts and maintain a small profile. Propagate by separation of the root.

Japanese chrysanthemum (kangiku, *Chrysanthemum indicum*)

Daisy family. While usually one thinks of chrysanthemums as autumn-bloomers, there are in fact three other types, one that blooms in spring, one in summer, and one in winter, such as this.

CARE: Protect from rain, which easily causes disease, by keeping the plant sheltered or beneath the eaves. Shortage of water will cause the lower leaves to yellow.

HERBACEOUS PERENNIALS CONTINUED

Kuma bamboo grass (koguma-zasa, *Sasa veitchii*)

Grass family. This grass is an attractive plant with brightly colored, small-sized leaves.

CARE: Grow in a rather damp environment because this very fertile plant thrives in moist soil. It is resilient to cold as well, making it easy to grow. Since the plant propagates itself by rhizomes, only prune for height.

Round-leaved cyclamen *(Cyclamen coum)*

Myrsine family. This is the wild breed of cyclamen. Flowers and leaves are diminutive and very charming. Flowers may be any of a number of colors: white, pink, reddish purple, or other.

CARE: The plant does not do well in heat, so place in shade during the summer and reduce the amount of water. Move into the sunshine in fall. The plant resists cold well but needs to be protected from frost.

Thunberg spirea (pink yukiyanagi, *Spiraea thunbergii*)

Rose family. In spring, the bud and early bloom of this spirea are a lovely rosy color, becoming white as the blossom opens.

CARE: This hardy plant holds up well against both cold and heat. Grows in the sun as well as in partial shade. If you prune it right after blooming is over, you can train it to the size you want.

Variegated Mt. Fuji rockcress (fu-iri hatazao, *Arabis serrata* 'Variegata')

Cabbage family. This variegated rockcress with yellow-colored leaves grows in grasslands or sandy soils by the seacoast. A single stem grows straight up from the plant, and a cluster of small flowers appears at the tip.

CARE: Grow in partial shade. Place under the eaves or indoors during the winter, and protect from the summer sun with a blind or other shelter.

Variegated strawberry begonia (fu-iri yukinoshita, *Saxifraga stolonifera* 'Variegata')

Saxifrage family. This is a variety of saxifrage with white-patterned leaves. The entire stalk is covered with hairs; in the summertime numerous five-petaled white flowers appear.

CARE: The plant is not fond of heat and should be placed in a shady spot during the summer where it gets good ventilation. Propagate by root separation.

Metric Conversions

For purposes of this book, these are the rough metric equivalents of container sizes given in inches.

inches	*centimeters*
1/2	1.0
3/4	2.0
1	2.5
1 1/4	3.0
1 1/3	3.5
1 1/2	4.0
1 3/4	4.5
2	5.0
2 1/4	5.5
2 1/2	6.0
2 3/4	7.0
3	7.5
3 1/4	8.0
3 1/2	9.0
4	10
5	13
6	15
7	18
7 1/2	19
8	20
11 1/2	29
14	36

Resources

Mail-order suppliers of bonsai plants and materials

UNITED STATES

Bonsai by the Monastery
2625 Hwy 212 SW
Conyers, GA 30094
bonsaimonk.com
800-778-7687

Bonsai Superstore
14775 SW 232 St.
Miami, FL 33172
bonsaisuperstore.com
800-778-7687

California Bonsai Studio
4015 N. Moorpark Rd.
Thousand Oaks, CA 91360
californiabonsai.com
805-870-4187

Hollow Creek Bonsai
2124 Dutch Hollow Rd.
Avon, NY 14414
hollowcreekbonsai.com
585-734-7035

Maiban Bonsai
550 S. Van Ness Ave., #303
San Francisco, CA 94110
maibanbonsai.com
800-231-9592

New England Bonsai Garden
914 South Main St.
Bellingham, MA 02019
nebonsai.com
508-883-2842

Sanderson Creek Bonsai
1634 Stella St.
Fort Worth, TX 76104
sandersonbonsai.com
817-534-3220

Soh-Ju-En Satsuki Bonsai
2254 Tennessee St.
Vallejo, CA 94591
sohjuensatsukibonsai.com
707-315-5492

Stone Lantern
PO Box 70
Passumpsic, VT 05861
stonelantern.com
800-776-1167

Wee Tree Farm
PO Box 340
Philomath, OR 97370
weetree.com
541-929-9520

CANADA

Misho Bonsai
337 St-James
Gatineau, Québec J8P 3N7
mishobonsai.com
818-669-6476

UNITED KINGDOM

British Bonsai
Chetwynd
Hillsdale Walk
Storrington
West Sussex RH20 3HL
britishbonsai.com
07904 062369

Green Dragon Bonsai
Unit 9
The Old Depot
Trelawnyd
Denbighshire LL18 6DN
greendragonbonsai.co.uk
075 0000 5337

Bonsai Societies

American Bonsai Society
absbonsai.org

Federation of British Bonsai Societies
fobbsbonsai.co.uk

National Bonsai Society (U.K.)
thenationalbonsaisociety.co.uk

INDEX

SINAJINA

Located in a quiet neighborhood, the shop sells wildflowers in season and provides garden design services. A showroom displays a wide array of keshiki bonsai arrangements, for viewing and for sale. Classes are also offered.

B 2-35-13 Okuzawa
Setagaya Tokyo
158-0083

Business hours:
10 a.m. – 7 p.m.
Closed Wednesday
sinajina.com